Use R!

Series Editors:
Robert Gentleman   Kurt Hornik   Giovanni Parmigiani

For further volumes:
http://www.springer.com/series/6991

Wolfgang Jank

Business Analytics for Managers

 Springer

Wolfgang Jank
Department of Decision and Information Technologies
Robert H. Smith School of Business
University of Maryland
Van Munching Hall
College Park, MD 20742-1815
USA
wjank@rhsmith.umd.edu

Series Editors:
Robert Gentleman
Program in Computational Biology
Division of Public Health Sciences
Fred Hutchinson Cancer Research Center
1100 Fairview Avenue, N. M2-B876
Seattle, Washington 98109
USA

Kurt Hornik
Department of Statistik and Mathematik
Wirtschaftsuniversität Wien
Augasse 2-6
A-1090 Wien
Austria

Giovanni Parmigiani
The Sidney Kimmel Comprehensive
Cancer Center at Johns Hopkins University
550 North Broadway
Baltimore, MD 21205-2011
USA

ISBN 978-1-4614-0405-7   e-ISBN 978-1-4614-0406-4
DOI 10.1007/978-1-4614-0406-4
Springer New York Dordrecht Heidelberg London

Library of Congress Control Number: 2011934258

Printed on acid-free paper

Springer is part of Springer Science+Business Media (www.springer.com)

To my Family:

*Angel, Isabella, Alexander, Waltraud,
Gerhard, and Sabina*

Preface

This book is about analytics and data-driven decision making. As such, it could easily be mistaken for a book on statistics or data mining. In fact, this book conveys *ideas* and *concepts* from both statistics and data mining, with the goal of extracting knowledge and actionable insight for managers. However, this is not a statistics book. There exist thousands of books on the topic of statistics. Most of these books are written by statisticians *for* statisticians. As a result, they often focus primarily on mathematics, formulas, and equations and not so much on the practical insight that can be derived from these equations. This book *uses* concepts and ideas from statistics (without ever getting bogged down in too much mathematical detail) in order to extract insight from real business data.

This is also not a book on data mining. There are many good data mining books, some of which are written for data miners and computer scientists, others for practitioners. However, most of these books focus on algorithms and computing. That is, they emphasize the many different algorithms that exist in order to extract similar information from the same set of data. This book does not emphasize algorithms. In fact, it acknowledges early on that while there may exist many different ways to solve and tackle a particular problem, the goal is to convey only the main principles of how to discover new knowledge from data and how to make data-driven decisions in a smart and informed way.

And finally, this is also not a book on software. While this book provides in its final chapter a quick-start to one of the most powerful software solutions, emphasis is placed on conveying data-driven *thinking* (and not so much on implementation). The ideas discussed in this book can be implemented using many different software solutions from many different vendors. In fact, this book purposefully steers clear of software implementation since it is our experience that books that do discuss software often place too much emphasis on implementation details, which confuses readers and distract them from the main point. After all, the main point of this book is *not* to train new statisticians or data miners – there are better books that can accomplish that goal. The main point is to convey the use and value of data-driven decision making to managers. Managers hardly ever implement complex methods and models themselves – however, they frequently communicate with personnel who do. With that in mind, the main goals of this book are as follows:

- To excite managers and decision makers about the *potential* that resides in data and the *value* that data analytics can add to business processes.
- To provide managers with a basic understanding of the main concepts of data analytics and a common language to convey data-driven decision problems so they can better communicate with personnel specializing in data mining or statistics.

After all, we are living in an information-based society, and using that information smartly can have benefits to both the business and the consumer.

January 2011   Wolfgang Jank

Contents

Chapter 1
Introduction

1.1 Analytics and Business

The practice of business is changing. More and more companies are amassing larger and larger amounts of data, storing them in bigger and bigger databases. Every day, telephone companies are collecting several *terabytes* of data about who we call, when we call them, and how long we talk to them. Every time we scan our *loyalty card* at a grocery store, we provide valuable information about the products we like, when we consume them, and the price we are willing to pay for them. In fact, data collection has become particularly valuable for understanding the relationship between price and demand. Large Consumer-to-Consumer (C2C) online auction sites (such as eBay or uBid) own immense treasure chests of price and demand data as they observe individuals' willingness to pay (i.e., individuals' bids) as well as product supply (i.e., auction inventories) and demand (i.e., the proportion of auctions that transact), dispersed both geographically (i.e., across different markets and nations) and temporally (i.e., across economically or seasonally changing environments).

The Internet is a particularly convenient place for data collection: every time we click on a link or visit a new Website, we leave a *digital footprint* (e.g., in the form of "cookies" or other tracking devices), thus allowing marketers to assemble a complete picture of our browsing behavior (and, ultimately, our personality and purchasing preferences). While this trove of personal information has led to some concerns about consumers' privacy,[1] it can be put to use in ways that are beneficial for all (rather than only select individuals or businesses). Take the example of Internet search engines (such as Google or Yahoo). Google analyzes the information from millions of individual Websites and how they "vote" on each other's usefulness. Then, sorting through the network of relationships among millions and millions of Websites, it returns the most relevant results every time we

---

[1] See online.wsj.com/article/SB10001424052748703940904575395073512989404.html.

W. Jank, *Business Analytics for Managers*, Use R!, DOI 10.1007/978-1-4614-0406-4_1,

search. In fact, Google mines the billions of searches it receives every day in such an efficient way that it can anticipate what we are searching for before we type it (and often automatically corrects our spelling). Internet search engines are a particularly compelling example of the power of information: every time we submit a search to Google, we tell it our most private secrets. In fact, we may tell it that we are looking for a new job or that we are seriously ill – Google knows about it even when no one else in the world does! While such information can be subject to abuse when placed into the wrong hands, it can lead to benefits for the entire society. For instance, Google mines searches related to the flu[2] and is able to anticipate outbreaks earlier than conventional methods, which can help policy makers in epidemiology or health care make timelier and more accurate decisions.

Data mining is particularly important for companies that only operate online (such as Amazon or Netflix). The reason is that these companies never meet their customers in person and thus do not have the ability to observe their behavior or directly ask them about their needs. Thus, the ability to deduce customers' preferences from their browsing behavior is key for online retailers. Indeed, Amazon carefully analyzes a user's past transactions (together with transactions from other users) in order to make recommendations about new products. For instance, it may recommend to us a new book (based on other books we have purchased in the past) or a product accessory (based on the accessories other customers have bought). If these recommendations match a user's preferences and needs, then there is a higher chance of a new transaction – and increased sales for Amazon! Automated and data-driven recommendations (also known as *recommendation engines*[3]) have become the Holy Grail for many Internet retailers. The immense value of recommendation engines can be seen particularly in the example of Netflix, which paid 1 million dollars to a team of scientists who improved their in-house recommendation engine by 10%.[4]

The collection and analysis of data is important not only on the Internet – it is equally important for more traditional (e.g., brick-and-mortar) businesses. Take the example of the credit card industry (or other credit-granting industries, such as mortgage and banking or the insurance industry). Credit card issuers often experience *adverse selection*[5] in the sense that those consumers who want their products most eagerly are often the ones who also carry the highest risk. Indeed, the reason that a person is desperate for a new credit card may be that he has an extremely bad credit score and no other company is willing to issue him a credit card. On the other hand, people who already own two or three credit cards (and have a stellar credit score) may be rather unlikely to respond to a new credit card offer. So, do we want that person who responds to our offer in a rather eager and desperate fashion as our new customer? This is exactly the situation that Capital One faced several

---

[2] See http://www.google.org/flutrends/.

[3] See http://en.wikipedia.org/wiki/Recommender_system.

[4] See http://www.netflixprize.com/.

[5] See http://en.wikipedia.org/wiki/Adverse_selection.

years ago when it entered the credit card market. As a new company, it wanted to gain market share quickly. However, there was also a danger that those customers who were willing to switch most quickly were also the most risky ones. In order to respond to these challenges, Capital One created a new (and innovative, at that time) *information-based strategy* in which they conducted thousands of laboratory-like experiments in order to better understand what characteristics distinguish good customers from bad. Moreover, they also carefully mined customers' behavior, such as the way in which a customer responded to a credit card offer. For instance, a customer responding via phone would be flagged as a little more risky than one who assembled a written response sent via regular mail.

Successful applications of data-driven decision making in business are plentiful and are increasing on a daily basis. Harrah's Casinos uses data analytics not only to record their customers' past activities but especially to predict future behavior. In fact, Harrah's can predict a customer's *potential* net worth (i.e., how much money they would be gambling per visit and how often they would be visiting over their lifetime) based on data mining techniques. Using that net worth analysis, they create custom advertising messages and special offer packages for each customer. Data mining can also help tap into the "pulse" of the nation (or the consumer). By analyzing sentiments (e.g., positive vs. negative opinions) over thousands of blogs,[6] companies can obtain real-time information about their brand image. This could be particularly important when products face problems (e.g., car recalls) or for identifying new product opportunities (e.g., sleeper movies at the box office).

The list of successful data mining stories goes on. AT&T uses *social network analysis* (i.e., mining the links and nodes in a network) to identify fraud in their telephone network. Automated and data-driven fraud detection is also popular with credit card companies such as Visa and Mastercard. Large accounting companies (such as PriceWaterhouse) develop data-driven methods to unearth inconsistencies in accounting statements. Other companies (such as IBM) use internal as well as external data in order to predict a customer's "wallet" (i.e., their potential for purchasing additional services). And the list goes on. More curious examples include human resource management at successful sports teams. For instance, both the Boston Red Sox (baseball) and the New England Patriots (football) are famous for using data analytics to make decisions about the composition of their teams. All of this shows that data can play a key role and can provide a competitive edge across many different sectors and in many different business processes (both internal and external).

1.2 Goal of This Book

The common theme across all of these aforementioned cases and examples is that they rely on the collection and analysis of data in order to make better business decisions. Thus, the goal of this book is to convey the value of data-driven analytics

---

[6]See, for example, http://www.blogpulse.com/.

to managers and business students. This book is very hands-on and practice-oriented. In fact, while there are many books on the topic of statistics and data mining, only a few are written in a way accessible to managers. Many books get lost in mathematical and algorithmic detail rather than focusing on the role of data mining for solving real business problems. This book will take a very pragmatic approach. Starting with actual decision-making problems, this book will motivate the need for data and data-driven solutions by using real data from real business scenarios. Starting from basic principles, the reader will learn about the importance of data exploration and visualization, and understand different methods for data modeling. Emphasis will be placed on understanding when to use which method.

This book will also allow managers to better interact with personnel specializing in analytics. In fact, the goal of this book is *not* to train new statisticians and data miners – there are many other books that will accomplish this goal. The goal is to expose managers and decision makers to the key ideas and concepts of data-driven decision making. In that sense, the goal is not to be exhaustive in every single detail of data mining and statistics but to motivate the need for data-driven decision making and to provide managers with the necessary background and vocabulary to successfully *interact* with specialized personnel trained in data mining or statistics.

1.3   Who Should Read This Book?

This book is geared toward business students and managers who are looking to obtain a competitive "edge" via analytics. With increasing desktop computing power and companies amassing massive amounts of data, business decisions are becoming more and more data-based. This holds in many sectors, but in particular in banking, insurance, investments, retailing, electronic commerce, advertising, and direct marketing. Because of this new approach to business, companies are in need of people with a new set of computational skills. There is also an increasing notion that in order to stay competitive, managers need to be re-equipped with long-lost analytical skills. In fact, there is often a disconnect between the people who run analytics (such as statisticians, data miners, and computer scientists) and management (who may have a background in marketing or finance but not very much technical training). This disconnect often stems from the fact that the two groups "do not speak the same language." While the technical folks talk in terms of algorithms and bytes, the business folks think about investments and returns. One goal of this book is to provide management with a better appreciation of the value of data analytics. In doing so, it will also provide a platform for a "joint language" in that it will make it easier for management to appreciate and understand analytical efforts.

1.4   What This Book Is *Not*

1.4.1   *This Is Not a Statistics Book*

Most books on statistics put mathematics and mathematical formulas at their center. This book is purposefully clean of mathematics and formulas. This is not to say that mathematics is unimportant – on the contrary, mathematics plays an important role in the development of statistical models and methods. However, the focus in this book is not on the development of statistical methods but rather on the *application* of statistical thinking to business problems. Based on our own teaching experience, too much mathematical detail often confuses (and sometimes even scares) the inexperienced and novice user of statistical methods. Therefore, the goal of this book is to explain statistical concepts mainly in plain English, abstaining from the use of mathematical symbols and equations as much as possible. We are aware that this approach can sometimes lead to statements and explanations that are slightly imprecise (at least in a mathematical sense), but our overarching goal is to train business leaders and managers to appreciate statistics and to adopt the findings of data-driven decision making into their own language. Thus a treatment of analytics in plain English is essential.

1.4.2   *This Is Not a Data Mining Book*

This is also not a traditional data mining book. Most data mining books focus on the trained expert (either from computer science, statistics, or mathematics) and as such emphasize algorithms and methods over intuition and business insight. Most data mining books also cover a wide range of data mining algorithms, such as neural networks, trees, or support vector machines. The focus in this book is not so much on the many different algorithms that are available (many of them tackling similar problems, such as classification or prediction) but rather on the differences in data and business scenarios that require different types of analytical approaches and ideas. As such, this book will not provide the same breadth of coverage of different algorithms as traditional data mining books. Instead, it will focus on a few select algorithms and models and explain the differences they make for business decision making.

1.5   What This Book *Is*

So, what is this book? Well, probably the best answer is that we envision this book to be a valuable resource for business students and managers who do not have much of a background in statistics or mathematics but who wish to get a better appreciation of data and data-driven decision making. This book focuses a lot on intuition and insight. It discusses many different data scenarios and related business questions that might arise. Then, it illustrates different ways of extracting new business knowledge from this data. The emphasis is on using plain English and conveying often complex mathematical concepts in "layman's terms." We envision that this book could be used in a first course on business analytics for MBA students or in executive education programs. This book is not exhaustive in that it does not cover everything that there is to know when it comes to data mining for business. We believe that knowing every single detail cannot be the goal for a manager. Rather, our goal is to communicate concepts of statistics and data mining in nonthreatening language, to create excitement for the topic, and to illustrate (in a hands-on and very concrete fashion) how data can add value to the everyday life of business executives.

1.6   Structure of This Book

The structure of this book is as follows. In Chapter 2, we introduce data exploration. By data exploration we mean both numerical and graphical ways of understanding the data. Data exploration is probably the single most important step of any data analysis – yet, it is also the least appreciated and most neglected one. The reason is that with the availability of powerful algorithms embedded into user-friendly software, most users will jump directly into building complex models and methods without ever getting a clear understanding of their data. We will spend quite some time discussing a wide array of data explorations in Chapter 2. The reason is that data can be very complex – in fact, chances are that our data is more complex and complicated than we initially believed. Unleashing powerful algorithms and methods on such data can have detrimental results, ranging from inaccurate predictions to complete meaninglessness of our results. Hence, we advocate that data needs to be explored first in a very careful manner. In fact, we like to think of the data exploration step as "diving" into our data and investigating it from the inside out. Only when we can be sure that we understand every single detail of our data (patterns, trends, unusual observations, and outliers) can we apply models and methods with peace of mind.

Subsequent chapters cover different aspects of data modeling. We start in Chapter 3 by introducing basic modeling ideas. By "basic" we mean answers to fundamental questions such as "What is a model?" and "Why do we need models at all?" We also introduce the most basic concept of estimating a model from data via least squares regression. We discuss model interpretation and evaluation and distinguish statistical significance of the results from practical relevance.

In Chapter 4, we introduce a few key ideas to make models more flexible. Our initial (basic) model may not be flexible enough because it assumes "linearity": it assumes that growth (or decay) occurs at a never-changing constant rate. Clearly, this may not be appropriate in all business scenarios: we may be willing to believe that sales grow as we increase our marketing efforts, but will sales grow at the same rate regardless of how much money we spend on marketing? Could it be that we reach a "saturation point" (or a point of diminishing returns) from which additional expenditures on marketing will return a smaller increment in sales? If so, then we should worry about making our model flexible enough – and the precise details are covered in Chapter 4.

In Chapter 5, we cover yet another important aspect of model building: making models selective. The novice user of statistics and data mining tools often gets overly excited by the power of data and soon thinks that "more is better." What we mean by that is that inexperienced users often have the perception that the more data we "throw" at our model, the better the result. While it is certainly important to have "enough" data, using too much information can result in inferior outcomes. For instance, while we may think that using aggregate household characteristics in addition to marketing expenditures will result in a better forecasting model for sales, this is not an automatic conclusion. What if our marketing expenditures are allocated *as a function* of household characteristics? For instance, what if we had decided to allocate more marketing resources in zip codes with higher median household incomes? Would household income then still add value for modeling sales? Would it contain much additional information above and beyond the information that already resides in marketing expenditures? The answer is "No." Since household characteristics would be strongly correlated with marketing expenditures, it would not make much sense to include both in the same model (at least in this hypothetical example). In Chapter 5, we will discuss different approaches for selecting "good" (or useful) information and weeding out the "bad" (or less useful) information.

In Chapter 6, we will discuss a few additional ideas that we refer to as "fine-tuning" our model. There are many different approaches for fine-tuning one's model, and new approaches are being invented every day in the academic literature of statistics and data mining. What we will focus on in this chapter are a few established approaches that will help overcome some of the lingering shortcomings of the previous chapters. These shortcomings are (a) the difference between a model's explanatory power and predictive capability and (b) the ability to capture any kind of (complex) relationship.

1.7   Using This Book in a Course

While this book can be used as stand-alone reading material, we have taught similar material in eight-week courses for both MBA and executive education students. A possible course sequence could be as follows:

Lecture 1   Data exploration, visualization, and discovery (Chapter 2)

Lecture 2   Basic modeling concepts, least squares regression, and interpretation (Sections 3.1, 3.2)

Lecture 3 Statistical vs. practical significance and identifying important predictors (Section 3.3)

Lecture 4 More flexible models (1): Dummy variables and interaction terms (Section 4.1)

Lecture 5 More flexible models (2): Data transformations and nonlinear relationships (Section 4.2)

Lecture 6 The danger of too much information and making models more selective (Chapter 5)

Lecture 7 Assessing a model's capabilities: explanatory vs. predictive power (Section 6.1)

Lecture 8 Modeling more complex relationships via nonparametric methods (Section 6.2)

Chapter 2
Exploring and Discovering Data

In this chapter, we discuss different approaches for exploring data. Data exploration is probably the single most important step in any data analysis. While the availability of huge amounts of data often tempts the user to jump directly into sophisticated models and methods, one of the main messages of this book is that it is of extreme importance to first understand one's data and to thoroughly explore it for patterns and anomalies.

So, why do we perform data exploration? The answer is very simple: to better understand our data and get intimately familiar with it. We simply should not base business decisions on complex methods and models unless we are certain that these methods capture the essence of our data. For instance, much of this book will talk about *linear* models. But what if the reality is not quite linear? What if our business processes are subject to "diminishing returns"? How could we detect such "non-linearities"? We could have a "hunch" that our process requires a somewhat different model, but sometimes (especially when dealing with new business processes) we simply don't know. But, as it turns out, our data typically knows much more about our processes than we do, and data exploration will tease out all of its knowledge. Moreover, data exploration is useful not only to detect trends and patterns but is equally important for uncovering anomalies and outliers. Not every single one of our customers behaves in the same way. In fact, there are typically a few customers who behave in ways very different from the bulk of our customers. It is important that we can identify such customers and deal with them in the appropriate way. Data exploration will help us pick out such atypical customers and their behavior.

In this chapter, we present an array of data exploration methods and tools. In Section 2.1, we start with *basic* data summaries and visualizations. We use the word "basic" since they should be part of everyone's toolset and should be consulted every single time we explore new data. These basic tools include summary statistics (such as the mean, median, or mode), frequency tables, and histograms and boxplots for exploring the distribution of variables, as well as scatterplots, correlation tables, and cross-tabulations for exploring pairwise relationships among variables.

W. Jank, *Business Analytics for Managers*, Use R!, DOI 10.1007/978-1-4614-0406-4_2,
© Springer Science+Business Media, LLC 2011

Many of these basic tools discussed in Section 2.1 can be found in spreadsheets (such as Excel) and are not necessarily a special or distinguishing feature of specialized data mining software. In subsequent sections, though, we also discuss "more advanced" (or more powerful) tools for data exploration. Many of these advanced tools cannot be found in spreadsheets, and they illustrate the power of more advanced data mining solutions. To that end, we will discuss scatterplot matrices and trellis graphs (Section 2.2), time series graphs (Section 2.3), spatial graphs (Section 2.4), density and spine plots for categorical responses (Section 2.5), or a combination of several different types of graphs and data-aggregation techniques for panel data (Section 2.6).

We also want to emphasize that, in contrast to many standard textbooks on statistics, we do not explicitly separate *numerical* data summaries (such as the mean or the standard deviation) from *graphical* displays (e.g., a histogram) since we believe that both numerical and visual data exploration should be used simultaneously, as one informs the other and their joint and simultaneous application leads to better insight about patterns and anomalies in the data.

2.1 Basic Data Summaries and Visualizations: House Price Data

We start out by discussing some of the most basic tools for exploring data. We use the word "basic" because these approaches constitute the minimum toolset that each analyst should possess. They also can often be found in spreadsheets and are therefore in widespread use. Either way, mastering these tools is an absolute must!

Data: Table 2.1 shows a sample of house prices (and associated house characteristics) for a major US metropolitan area. In particular, it shows a house's ID, its selling price (in US$), its size (in square feet), the number of bedrooms and bathrooms, the

Table 2.1 The house price data. See also file `HousePrices.csv`.

ID	Price	SqFt	#Beds	#Baths	Offers	Brick	Nbhd
1	114300	1790	2	2	2	No	East
2	114200	2030	4	2	3	No	East
3	114800	1740	3	2	1	No	East
4	94700	1980	3	2	3	No	East
5	119800	2130	3	3	3	No	East
6	114600	1780	3	2	2	No	North
7	151600	1830	3	3	3	Yes	West
8	150700	2160	4	2	2	No	West
9	119200	2110	4	2	3	No	East

number of offers it has received while being on the market, whether or not it has brick walls,[1] and the neighborhood where it is located.[2]

Goal: One of the main goals of this analysis is to determine what drives the price of a house. For instance, it is reasonable to assume that larger houses (i.e., those with larger square footage) will fetch a higher price. But *how much more* does the price increase for each additional square foot? Also, does the siding material (i.e., brick vs nonbrick) have a significant impact on price? Or, does it matter in which neighborhood the house is located? Answers to these questions could help a potential buyer decide how much to bid for a house. It could also help the seller (or his realtor) price the house properly.

We accomplish this goal in several steps. First, we investigate the *distribution* of individual variables. For instance, we investigate *summary statistics* such as the average (or median) price to obtain a general sense of a typical home's value. We also compute the standard deviation of price to understand how much house prices are fluctuating around that typical value; high fluctuations could be indicative of a market in which it is hard to compare the value of one home with that of another home (which may be an advantage for the seller). We compute the *histogram* of price in order to gauge the shape of the price distribution, which could help us determine whether there exist unusual homes (with unusually high or low values). After investigating the distribution of all variables *individually*, we look at *pairwise relationships*. Pairwise relationships let us understand whether, for example, the price of a house increases with its square footage, or whether an additional bedroom has a stronger impact on price than an additional bathroom. Pairwise relationships are explored using *correlation measures* or *scatterplots*. We advocate the use of both correlations and scatterplots simultaneously since each conveys different pieces of the (big) picture: while scatterplots allow us to determine whether there exists any (practically relevant) relationship and the *form* of that relationship, correlation measures allow us to quantify (and hence compare) the strength of this correlation. We start out by discussing summary statistics for the house price data in more detail.

Summary Statistics: Table 2.2 shows summary statistics for the house price data. In particular, we compute the minimum (Min) and the maximum (Max), the first and third quartiles (1st Qu and 3rd Qu), the median and the mean (or average), and the standard deviation (StDev).

Looking at the first column of Table 2.2, we can learn that the average (or mean) house price equals $130,427. We can also see that house prices are slightly *skewed* since the mean price is a bit larger than its median value ($125,950). The most and least expensive houses sold for $211,200 (Max) and $69,100 (Min), respectively. The first quartile ($111,325) implies that 25% of all homes have sold for *less* than $111,325; similarly, the third quartile implies that 25% of homes have sold for *more* than $148,250, so there is considerable variability in house prices. In fact,

---

[1] Many homes in the United States have vinyl or other types of siding.

[2] Neighborhoods in this data are characterized as East, North, or West.

Table 2.2 Summary statistics for the house price data.

	Price	SqFt	#Beds	#Baths	Offers
Min	69100	1450	2.00	2.00	1.00
1st Qu	111325	1880	3.00	2.00	2.00
Median	125950	2000	3.00	2.00	3.00
Mean	130427	2001	3.02	2.45	2.58
StDev	26869	211	0.73	0.51	1.07
3rd Qu	148250	2140	3.00	3.00	3.00
Max	211200	2590	5.00	4.00	6.00

Table 2.3 Frequency table for *Brick* and *Neighborhood*.

Variable	Categories		
Brick	No	Yes	
	86	42	
Neighborhood	East	North	West
	45	44	39

the standard deviation ($26,869) measures the precise amount of this variability. One way to interpret the standard deviation is as follows: if house prices were perfectly symmetrically distributed around their mean, then a standard deviation of $26,869 implies that 95% of all house prices fall within $130,427 $\pm 2 \times$ $26,869$, (i.e., between $76,689 and $184,165), a considerable range. The general formula for this relationship is *Mean* $\pm 2 \times$ *StDev*. Of course, before applying this formula, we have to check first whether the distribution is in fact symmetric around the mean. We can do this using, for example, a histogram of price (see below).

We can also learn from Table 2.2 that the typical house has three bedrooms and between two and three bathrooms. (Notice that while the median number of baths equals 2, its mean is 2.45, which suggests that there are a few "outliers" with a surprisingly large number of bathrooms; in fact, the largest number of bathrooms (Max) in our data equals 4.) The typical house also has a size of 2,000 square feet, and it appears that the variability in home size (standard deviation = 211 SqFt) is not very high. And finally, we learn that most homes get between two and three offers; however, there also exist some rather unusual homes that have received as many as six offers.

Frequency Tables: Note that while there are a total of seven different data columns available ("compare" Table 2.1), Table 2.2 shows summary statistics for only five of them. The reason lies in the differences in data types: while the first five columns are all *numerical* (i.e., measured on an interval scale), the last two columns are *categorical* (e.g., "Brick" assumes the values "Yes" or "No" but no numbers). We cannot compute summary statistics (such as the mean or the standard deviation) for nonnumeric data. Instead, we explore categorical data using *frequency tables* that compare the frequencies between individual categories. For instance, Table 2.3 shows that most houses (i.e., over 67%) are built from nonbrick material.

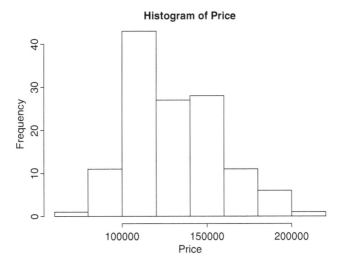

Fig. 2.1 Histogram of price.

Histograms: While summary statistics are a great way to summarize important aspects about a distribution in a single number, they are limited because they only capture a single aspect of that distribution. Most of the time, data are too complex to be summarized by a single number only. For instance, while the typical house in our data sells for $130,427, the price distribution could be skewed (i.e., there could be some houses that sell for much more), it could be multimodal (i.e., there could be not just one "typical" house but two or even three typical houses), there could be outliers (i.e., some houses that sell for an exorbitantly larger amount), or there could be other anomalies that cannot be detected using only a single number. To that end, we want to visualize the entire data distribution. This can be done using a histogram.

Figure 2.1 shows a histogram of price. We can see that the distribution appears rather symmetric around its mean, although there appears to be an unusual "bump" between $100,000 and $120,000. This suggests that while the "typical" house sells for $130,427, there is a rather large proportion that sell for significantly less.

Figure 2.2 shows histograms for the other numerical variables from Table 2.1. We can see that while the distribution of a home's size (i.e., square footage) is very symmetric, the distributions of the remaining three variables are skewed. For instance, while the average number of bathrooms is 2.45, there are some (but few) houses with as many as four bathrooms. Similarly, while a house typically receives 2.58 offers, some receive as many as six offers. We also want to point out that in the context of *discrete variables*, the average may not always be a meaningful way of summarizing data. For instance, note that the variable "number of bathrooms" assumes only discrete values (i.e., a house can have either 2 or 3 bathrooms but not 2.5). Thus, concluding that "the average number of bathrooms equals 2.58" does not make much sense. We can interpret this as the average house having between

Fig. 2.2 Histogram of other
numerical variables.

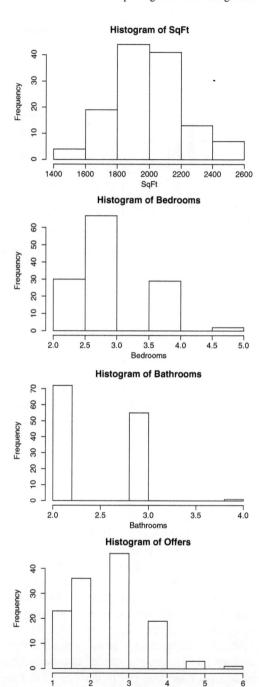

Fig. 2.3 Boxplot of price.

two and three bathrooms. Alternatively, the *median* tells us that a typical house has two bathrooms. The median is not affected by the difference between discrete and continuous data, and thus provides meaningful answers in both cases.

Boxplots: An alternative way of visualizing the entire distribution of a single variable is via *boxplots*. A boxplot graphs the *quartiles* of a distribution. That is, it draws a "box" between the first and third quartiles and marks the median by a vertical line inside that box. Furthermore, it draws "whiskers" between the outside of the boxes and 1.5 times the *interquartile range*; the interquartile range is the distance between the first and third quartiles and can hence be used as a measure of variability in the data. Data points beyond the whiskers are considered *outliers* and are marked by circles.

Figure 2.3 shows the boxplot for price. It conveys information similar to the histogram in Figure 2.1. However, we can now see more clearly that the price distribution is slightly right-skewed. (Note the longer whisker to the right side of the box, and the larger area inside the box to the right of the median.) A right-skewed price distribution suggests that some sellers manage to fetch a significantly higher price for their home than the rest; from a seller's point of view, it would be important to understand what these successful sellers do in order to get such a price premium. We can also identify one potential outlier on the boxplot; this outlier marks a house with a price that is above and beyond the rest. In that sense, the boxplot conveys information similar to the histogram, but it presents this information in a more detailed fashion.

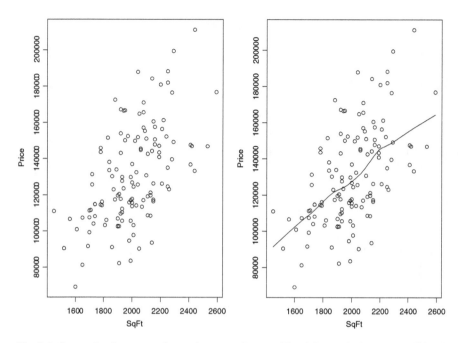

Fig. 2.4 Scatterplot between price and square footage. The left panel shows a traditional scatterplot displaying only the individual data points; the right panel shows an enhanced version with an overlaid smoothing line.

Scatterplots: After exploring each variable individually (using histograms, box-plots, and numerical summaries), we now want to investigate *pairwise relationships* between variables. The most common (and also most powerful) way of exploring pairwise relationships is via scatterplots. Scatterplots graph pairs of two variables' values on an *X*- and *Y*-coordinate system.

Figure 2.4 (left panel) shows a scatterplot between price and square footage. We can see that, unsurprisingly, there exists a positive relationship between the two (the larger the square footage, the larger the price). We can also see that this relationship appears almost *linear*; that is, it appears as if for every increase in square footage the price increases by the same (constant) amount. This observation will become important later on when our goal will be to *model* the relationship between price and square footage. The (almost) linear relationship between price and square footage becomes even more apparent in the right panel of Figure 2.4, which shows the same scatter of data points but with a smooth trend line overlaid.

While a scatterplot can be used to identify general trends, we can also use it to scrutinize individual data points. For instance, Figure 2.4 shows that while most houses have the same positive relationship between square footage and price, there are a few houses (at the top right corner of the graph) that appear to "fall off" that trend. Deviations from a general trend might be indicative of segments, pockets or geolocations that behave differently from the rest. Such segments or pockets are

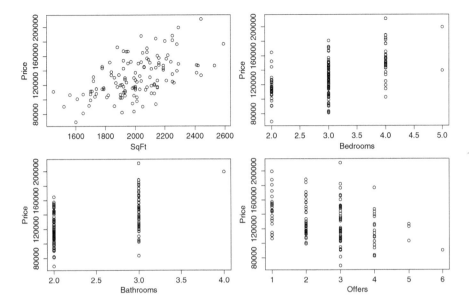

Fig. 2.5 Scatterplot between price and all four numerical variables.

important to identify, as we usually have to treat them with different marketing strategies (e.g., target different buyers, use different advertising or promotion strategies, etc.).

Figure 2.5 shows scatterplots between price and all four numerical variables. We can make several observations. First, while there exists a positive relationship between price and the number of bathrooms (and similarly for the number of bedrooms), the relationship between price and the number of offers appears negative. This last observation is curious since one may expect more offers to result in a higher level of competition, which, as one could argue, should result in a higher price. We also see that the scatterplots pertaining to the number of bathrooms and bedrooms are of rather limited use. In fact, since both variables assume only three and four different values, respectively, the information gleaned from the scatterplots is restricted. This illustrates that the use of scatterplots in connection with discrete variables should be done rather carefully.

Correlation Measures: While scatterplots provide a *graphical* way of investigating the relationship between pairs of variables, we can augment this graphical approach with a numerical assessment using pairwise *correlations*. In fact, while scatterplots are a great way of "seeing" relationships, the eye can sometimes betray us. Moreover, two people looking at the same graph may see two different patterns. It is thus often desirable to augment the visual (sometimes subjective) impressions gleaned from a scatterplot with objective numerical measures. Correlations provide such an objective measure.

Table 2.4 Correlations
between all numerical
variable.

	Price	SqFt	#Beds	#Baths	Offers
Price	1.00	0.55	0.53	0.52	−0.31
SqFt	0.55	1.00	0.48	0.52	0.34
#Beds	0.53	0.48	1.00	0.41	0.11
#Baths	0.52	0.52	0.41	1.00	0.14
Offers	−0.31	0.34	0.11	0.14	1.00

A correlation (also referred to as *Pearson's correlation*) measures the strength
and direction of the linear relationship between two variables. A large positive value
implies a strong positive relationship. It is important to remember that correlations
only capture *linear* relationships between two variables; that is, for two variables
that have a nonlinear relationship (e.g., curvilinear, circular, etc.), the correlation
may lead to wrong conclusions.

Table 2.4 shows the table of correlations between all five numerical variables
for the house price data. We point out again that since both "Brick" and "Neighborhood" are categorical, we cannot compute their correlation with price (at least
not directly). We can learn from Table 2.4 that price has the strongest positive
association with square footage (0.55) and that its correlation with the number
of bedrooms and bathrooms – while still positive – is weaker (0.53 and 0.52,
respectively). This illustrates one of the advantages of correlation measures over
scatterplots: while scatterplots also allow us to conclude that price has a positive
relationship with all three variables, we could not readily see which variable had the
strongest association with price. We again observe the negative relationship between
the number of offers and price, but we can now also see that this relationship is
not very strong (correlation = 0.33), so while the negative relationship is rather
surprising, it may actually not matter (at least not for all practical purposes).

Table 2.4 shows additional important information. For instance, we can see that
there is a rather strong correlation between square footage and the number of
bedrooms and bathrooms, respectively. This is not too surprising since one needs
a larger home in order to fit a larger number of rooms. However, this finding
also suggests that some of the information contained in square footage is already
captured by the number of bedrooms and bathrooms. This observation will become
important later on (we will refer to it as "multicollinearity") when we try to find
good models for price.

Cross-tabulations: We have pointed out repeatedly that computing numerical
summaries or correlations for categorical data is not possible (at least not directly).
One alternative to computing the correlation between two categorical variables
is to inspect their *cross-tabulation*. Table 2.5 shows the cross-tabulation between
brick and neighborhood. It appears that there is some relationship between the two
variables, as the percentage of brick homes in the North is significantly smaller
compared with the East (or the West). In fact, there exist alternative correlation
measures for categorical data. These measures are referred to as *Kendall's Tau*
or *Spearman's Rho*. For our data, Kendall's correlation between brick and
neighborhood equals −0.03 (and similarly for Spearman's correlation).

Table 2.5 Cross-tabulation
for *Brick* and *Neighborhood*.

	Neighborhood		
Brick	East	North	West
No	26	37	23
Yes	19	7	16

Lessons Learned:

- There exist several fundamentally different data types: numerical data vs. categorical data and continuous data vs. discrete data. Numerical data is recorded in the form of numbers and can be "measured"; categorical data is recorded in the form of classes or categories and it typically cannot be measured. Continuous data is numerical, which can be recorded on a "continuous scale" (i.e., with as many decimal places as desired); discrete data, on the other hand, only assumes a set of fixed (typically integer) data values. Depending on the data type, we need to apply different tools for data analysis and exploration. In particular, most tools for exploring numerical data do not work (at least not directly) for categorical data. In addition, certain summary statistics (e.g., the mean) may be more meaningful for continuous data and may require more careful interpretation when dealing with discrete data. The exploration of categorical data often needs special attention.

- There exist many different tools for exploring the distribution of a single variable. Among them are summary statistics (e.g. the mean, median, mode, standard deviation, minimum, and maximum), tables, or graphs (e.g., histograms and boxplots). All of these tools should be used jointly and simultaneously, as they complement one another. In fact, while graphs (such as a histogram) provide a visual impression of a distribution, they do not allow easy quantification (and hence make comparisons of two distributions challenging). Summary statistics explore distributions quantitatively and hence can be compared readily across two (or more) variables.

- There also exist many different tools for exploring relationships between pairs of variables. Among them are correlation measures, cross-tabulations, and scatterplots. As with tools for single variables, tools for exploring pairwise relationships complement one another and should be used simultaneously. While scatterplots provide a visual assessment of the relationship between two variables, correlation measures can quantify this relationship (and subsequently be used for comparison).

2.2   Data Transformations and Trellis Graphs:
Direct Marketing Data

In this section, we discuss a few more advanced and powerful ideas for exploring data. First, we introduce the concept of *scatterplot matrices*, which can unearth relationships between many different variables in one single graph. In fact, the version of scatterplot matrices that we use here is one of the most powerful available, as it combines scatterplots, correlation measures, and histograms in one single view. We also discuss data *transformation* as a means to obtain more consistent (and typically also more linear) relationship patterns. Then we discuss *trellis graphs*. Trellis graphs are powerful because they allow conditional views of the data. Trellis graphs are one of the most useful tools for unearthing new and unsuspected relationships in subsegments (or "pockets") of the data. It is often exactly these pockets that are of greatest value to the marketer or the investor, as they may offer opportunities that are otherwise impossible to detect.

Data: Table 2.6 shows data from a direct marketer. The direct marketer sells her products (e.g., clothing, books, or sports gear) only via direct mail; that is, she sends catalogs with product descriptions to her customers, and the customers order directly from the catalogs (via phone, Internet, or mail). The direct marketer is interested in mining her customers in order to better customize the marketing process. She is particularly interested in understanding what factors drive some customers to spend more money than others. To that end, she has assembled a database of customer records. These records include a customer's age (coded as young, middle, and old), gender (female/male), whether the customer owns or rents a home, whether the customer is single or married, the location of the customer relative to the nearest brick-and-mortar store that sells similar products (coded as far or close), the customer's salary (in US$), and how many children the customer has (between 0 and 3). The marketer also records the customer's past purchasing history (coded as low, medium, or high, or NA if the customer has not purchased anything in the past), the number of catalogs she has sent to that customer, and the amount of money the customer has spent (in US$).

Goal: One of the main goals of the marketer is to understand why some customers spend more than others. She is particularly interested in understanding the relationship between the number of catalogs and the amount of money spent since every catalog costs a fixed amount of money to produce and ship. Moreover, as the relationship with a customer matters, she is also interested in investigating whether customers with a high purchasing history in the past indeed also spend more money in the future. And lastly, as the marketer suspects that her product and service offerings may appeal more to some demographics than others, she is particularly interested in detecting "pockets" of customers that are most profitable (which she may ultimately decide to target with coupons and promotions).

 We again accomplish these goals using only exploratory tools (graphs and data summaries). Some of the tools we use here were introduced in Section 2.1, but here

Table 2.6 The direct marketing data. See also file `DirectMarketing.csv`.

Age	Gender	Home	Married	Loc	Sal	Chld	Hist	Ctlgs	Spent
Old	Female	Own	Single	Far	47500	0	High	6	755
Middle	Male	Rent	Single	Close	63600	0	High	6	1318
Young	Female	Rent	Single	Close	13500	0	Low	18	296
Middle	Male	Own	Married	Close	85600	1	High	18	2436
Middle	Female	Own	Single	Close	68400	0	High	12	1304
Young	Male	Own	Married	Close	30400	0	Low	6	495
Middle	Female	Rent	Single	Close	48100	0	Med	12	782
Middle	Male	Own	Single	Close	68400	0	High	18	1155

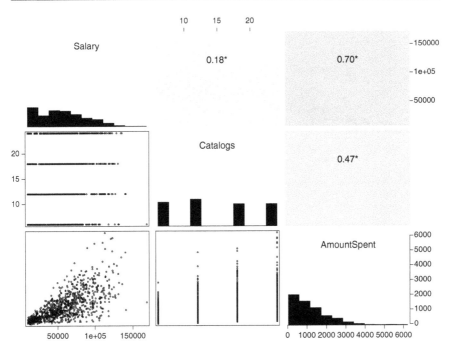

Fig. 2.6 Scatterplot matrix for salary, number of catalogs, and amount of money spent.

we use them in a slightly more advanced fashion. In addition, we also introduce new tools and concepts that are especially useful in the context of mining large databases. These include *scatterplot matrices*, *data transformations*, and *trellis graphs*.

Scatterplot Matrices: Figure 2.6 shows a scatterplot matrix for the variables salary, number of catalogs, and amount of money spent. In particular, it shows three different types of visualizations in one graph. Along the diagonal axis, it shows histograms for each of the three variables; below the diagonal, we see scatterplots between each of the three variable pairs; and above the diagonal we see the corresponding correlation values for each pair. Note that the correlation values are accompanied by different colorings, where darker colors indicate stronger correlations.

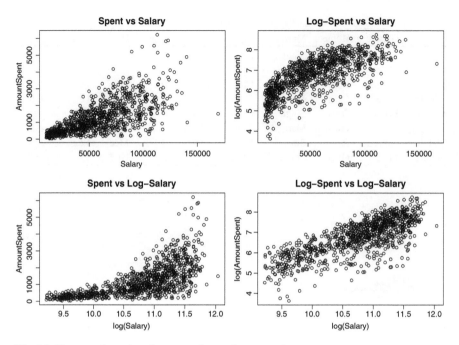

Fig. 2.7 Data transformations between salary and amount of money spent.

We can learn from Figure 2.6 that salary has the strongest correlation with the amount a customer spends. This is not too surprising because customers with little income are unlikely to spend a lot of money. But we can also learn that both salary and the amount spent are very right-skewed (notice the shape of the histograms) and, as a result, the relationship between the two is not at all consistent. In fact, if we look at the corresponding scatterplot (bottom left corner), then we notice that the points are "funneling out." In other words, while there is only a little variance at the lower levels of salary, the variance of amount spent increases with increasing levels of salary. An increasing variance is a problem because it implies that we cannot *predict* the spending behavior of the high-salary customers very accurately and, as a result, cannot target our potentially most profitable customers very well.

Data Transformations: Problems with skewed distributions in histograms or funnel effects in scatterplots can often be overcome (or at least smoothed out) by applying a suitable transformation to the data. Note that the scatterplot between salary and amount spent suggests that as salary and amount spent increase, the variation between the two also increases. We can eliminate this effect by transforming the data in a way that reels in the very large data values while leaving the smaller values unchanged. The logarithmic (or "log") transformation has this property. Figure 2.7 shows the changing relationship between salary and amount spent as we apply the log-transform to either salary, amount spent, or both. We can see that applying the log-transform to both salary and amount spent results in a

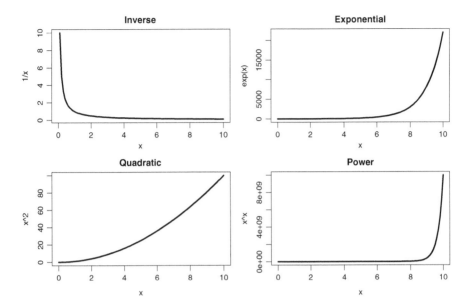

Fig. 2.8 Typical data transformation functions.

pattern that resembles a straight line. Moreover, the funnel effect has vanished; that is, the variation between the two variables is now the same at all levels. Thus, if we base our targeting efforts on the relationship between log-salary and log-spent, then we can target the high spenders with the same accuracy as the low spenders.

We have seen in the previous paragraph that a logarithmic transformation can ease data problems and in particular make relationships between variables more consistent. The logarithmic transformation is not the only transformation that can achieve that goal. There are many more transformations (such as exponential, inverse, quadratic, or the power transform) that can lead to similar results in different applications. Figure 2.8 illustrates some of these transformations.

Trellis Graphs: Our analysis thus far has revealed that there is a (linear) relationship between (log-) salary and (log-) amount spent; in other words, our most profitable customers will be the ones with the highest incomes. But does this relationship apply equally to all our customer segments? For instance, could it be that the rate at which customers spend their earnings varies between old and young customers? Figure 2.9 shows one answer to that question. It shows a *trellis graph*, which displays the relationship between two variables (log-salary and log-spent in this case) *conditioned* on one or more other variables (age and marital status in this case).

Figure 2.9 shows that the relationship between salary and amount spent varies greatly across different customer segments. While there is a strong linear relationship for old customers, there is almost no relationship for young married customers. In other words, while we can predict very accurately how much an old customer will

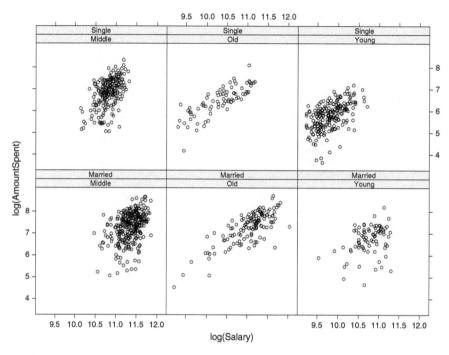

Fig. 2.9 Trellis graph for the direct marketing data. The relationship between salary and amount spent is conditioned on age and marital status.

spend, we cannot do the same for the young and married customers; we take this as an indication that it would be better to avoid this customer segment altogether. We can also see that compared with the previous two segments, the relationship for single middle-aged customers is much stronger (i.e., there is a much steeper trend, hence the rate of spending is much faster). Thus trellis graphs allow for a more granular inspection of the data and for the discovery of new segment-specific relationships. This is further illustrated in Figure 2.10, which shows another trellis graph, this time conditioned on a customer's spending history and location.

Lessons Learned:

- Scatterplot matrices allow us to visualize the relationships between many different pairs of variables on one single graph; they also allow us to incorporate additional information such as correlation values or the distribution of individual variables. Scatterplot matrices are a great tool for giving an overview of the most important data features in one single snapshot.
- Data transformations can be used to render more consistent relationships between variables. In fact, data transformations can be used to get rid of "funnel effects" or skew in variables. Data transformation includes

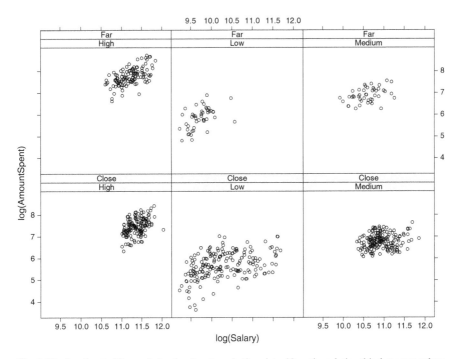

Fig. 2.10   Another trellis graph for the direct marketing data. Now the relationship between salary and amount spent is conditioned on purchasing history and location.

many different functional operators such as the logarithm or the quadratic function. The main goal of data transformation is to render the relationship more linear (i.e., to transform the data pattern so that it more-closely resembles a straight line).

- Trellis graphs allow us to investigate segment-specific relationships and detect pockets where relationships change. Unearthing this change of relationship could lead to a different managerial action: it could either lead to more specific, custom-made marketing or advertising, or it could lead to abandoning entire market segments altogether. In other words, trellis graphs allow us to detect pockets of opportunity and, equally, segments where no competitive edge exists.

2.3   Time Series Graphs: Soft Drink Sales Data

In this section, we discuss time series graphs. Time series graphs are different from the other visualizations discussed in this chapter, as they capture dynamic information that changes over time. While time series graphs are, at least in principle, a very simple concept, we discuss good and bad examples of them.

Table 2.7 Soft drink sales
data. See also file
`Softdrink.csv`.

Quarter	Sales	t	Q
Q1-86	1734.83	1	1
Q2-86	2244.96	2	2
Q3-86	2533.8	3	3
Q4-86	2154.96	4	4
Q1-87	1547.82	5	1
Q2-87	2104.41	6	2
Q3-87	2014.36	7	3
Q4-87	1991.75	8	4

Data: Table 2.7 shows a different kind of data. It shows sales (recorded in millions of dollars) of a major soft drink company. What makes this data different is that we only have two pieces of information available: information on the quarter (e.g., first quarter of 1986, Q1-86) and sales in that quarter. Note that Table 2.7 also has a quarter count t (which ranges from 1 to 56 since there are a total of 56 quarters in this data) and a quarter indicator Q, which denotes the quarter of the year (1 corresponds to the first quarter, 2 corresponds to the second quarter, etc.), but this is merely a recoding of the quarter information in the first column.

Goal: Our goal is to understand company sales, if and why they vary from quarter to quarter, and the rate at which they grow (or decay). Ultimately, a manager will want to use this information to *forecast* future sales for planning purposes. Specific items that we may want to identify are a *trend* (i.e., whether the data grows in a systematic pattern) and *seasonality* (i.e., whether that data fluctuates systematically; e.g., higher sales in the summer months and lower sales in winter).

Time Series Plot: While the data above appears to be rather simple (after all, it contains only two different pieces of information, time and sales), only a very careful analysis will reveal all the knowledge hidden in it. Figure 2.11 shows two different graphs of that data. The left panel shows a simple (scatter-) plot of sales versus time (quarter in this case). We can see that there appears to be a positive trend (sales grow over time), but we can also see that there appears to be a lot of noise around that trend. In fact, while sales appear to trend upward, individual data points scatter quite heavily around that trend. This would suggest that sales are quite variable from quarter to quarter, making sales forecasting quite burdensome and unreliable.

The right panel reveals the reason for this "noise." The colored boxes represent the type of quarter, and we can see that sales are generally higher in spring and summer (blue and green boxes) compared with fall and winter (light blue and red boxes). We can thus conclude that sales exhibit not only a positive trend but also a strong seasonal pattern. In other words, once we control for *both* trend and seasonality, the data aren't all that variable after all and there is good reason to believe that we can forecast sales quite accurately into the future.

We can make an additional observation: the dashed grey line shows a *smooth trend* through the data, and we can see that while sales are generally growing,

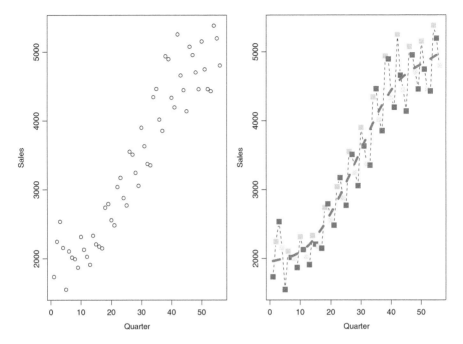

Fig. 2.11 Time series graphs for the soft drink sales data. The left panel shows a very simple graph of the data. In the right panel, colored boxes represent different quarters; the grey dotted line shows a smooth trend through the data.

the *rate of growth* is decreasing toward more recent quarters. In other words, sales increases are diminishing. Note that none of this information was directly obvious from the much simpler scatterplot in the left panel of Figure 2.11.

Lessons Learned:

- We can use time series graphs for visualizing trends and seasonality in data that is recorded over time. Time series data often appears dangerously simple when in fact it could hide a trove of valuable knowledge. This knowledge can be unearthed only by using the right graphical tools (such as color-coding different quarters differently or overlaying a smooth and flexible trend line). Time series data often shows a trend; that trend can be linear (i.e., growing at the same rate over time) or nonlinear. Nonlinear trends can occur in the form of increasing or decreasing growth rates and could capture real effects such as diminishing returns or an explosion of word-of-mouth referrals. Time series data can also show seasonality. Seasonality can occur on a quarter-to-quarter basis (e.g., summer vs. winter) or on a monthly basis. Seasonality can be detected more easily when it arrives in very regular patterns (e.g., winter sales are always lower

compared with spring sales). But seasonality can be less regular (and hence
a little harder to detect and capture). For instance, sales could bottom out in
January in one year but hit lows in February in the next year. While in both
years sales are lowest in the winter months (January or February), it is hard
to pinpoint the exact timing of the low on a year-to-year basis. Seasonality
can become even more complex (and hence harder to detect) when it occurs
only every few years. For instance, while the economy may grow in some
years, it may experience a downturn in other years. Such "ups and downs"
in long-term economic data are often referred to as cyclical (or business
cycle) rather than seasonal variations. From a modeling point of view, we
would need many years worth of data in order to properly account for such
business cycles.

2.4   Spatial Graphs: Online Purchase Preferences Data

We next discuss spatial graphs. By spatial graphs   we typically mean maps, and
we use them to visualize geographical dependencies. Spatial graphs are becoming
increasingly important with the increasing availability of spatial information. Take
for instance the very recent development of Google Latitude,[3] which allows Google
users to share their geographical locations. This is only one example, but it
suggests that geographical information on customers, products, or services will
explode in the upcoming years. Spatial information is extremely valuable because
it allows us to geotarget consumers. Local searches and searches on maps are only
two recent applications that rely heavily on geotargeting. Most spreadsheet-based
software packages (such as Excel) have no way of exploring geographical data.
This limitation does not allow managers to access and learn from one of the most
important pieces of business information.

Data: Table 2.8 shows data on geographical differences in product preferences
across the United States. The table shows sales data for books that were offered
both in print format and as downloadable PDF files (i.e., in electronic format). The
table also shows the price differences between print and PDF versions: PrPRINT
denotes the price of the print version (in US$); PrPDF denotes the corresponding
price of the PDF file. The electronic format was typically priced lower than the print
format, and RelPrPDF records the relative price difference between the two formats.
The table also records whether a customer purchased the PDF version (PurPDF) or

---

[3]See www.google.com/latitude.

Table 2.8 Geographical preference data. See also file `SpatialPreferences.csv`.

Long	Lat	PrPRINT	PrPDF	RelPrPDF	PurPDF	PurPRINT
−74.058	42.83326	34.95	17.48	50%	1	0
−163.11894	60.31473	39.95	29.96	75%	0	1
−163.11894	60.31473	39.95	29.96	75%	0	1
−86.1164	32.37004	28.00	7.00	25%	1	0
−111.82436	33.32599	24.95	18.71	75%	0	1
−111.82436	33.32599	18.00	13.5	75%	0	1
−118.29866	33.78659	49.95	0.00	0%	1	0
−118.29866	33.78659	57.95	14.49	25%	1	0

the (higher-priced) print version (PurPRINT).[4] Moreover, Long and Lat denote the longitude and latitude of the customer's location (i.e., it denotes the geographical area of the purchase).

Goal: One of the goals of the analysis is to determine whether there are geographical differences in product preferences. For instance, we may want to ask whether customers on the East Coast are more likely to purchase a book in the electronic format. Moreover, we would like to understand how product preferences vary as a function of the price difference between the print and PDF formats. Understanding customers' geographical preferences and price sensitivities allows retailers to better market their product, geotarget their customers, and offer the right coupons and promotions in the right locations.

Spatial Graphs: Figure 2.12 shows a map of the United States. On this map, we record the location of each transaction; a black circle represents a print purchase and a red circle represents a PDF purchase. The size of the circle corresponds to the price of the PDF for that relative to that of print. In other words, very large circles indicate that the PDF version was priced (almost) as high as the corresponding printed book; small circles indicate that the PDF version was available at a steep discount relative to the print version.

We can see that the preference between PDF and print varies significantly throughout the united states. While in some areas (e.g., in the South) print was the predominant format (unless the PDF was offered at a steep discount), in other areas (e.g., the West Coast or the Northeast) customers preferred the PDF format, even at a higher price. This insight can help marketing managers determine the right price for their product, geotarget their customers, and offer spatially varying coupons and promotions.

---

[4]We only show the transactions that resulted in either a print or a PDF purchase; of course, some transactions resulted in no purchase, but we do not show such data here.

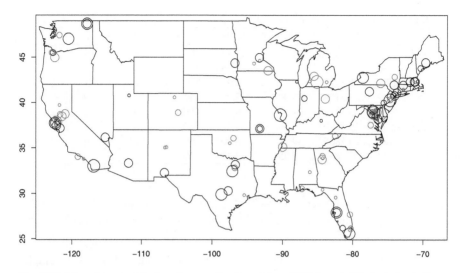

Fig. 2.12 Map of geographical preferences for the print vs. PDF format. Black circles indicate print purchases; red circles indicate PDF purchases. The size of the circle represents the price of PDF relative to print.

Lessons Learned:

- Spatial graphs, in particular maps, can be used for exploring geotagged data; that is, data with geographical information attached. Spatial graphs can be used for geotargeting and identifying geographical pockets of varying consumer demand.

2.5   Graphs for Categorical Responses: Consumer-to-Consumer Loan Data

In this section, we take a spatial look at data where the outcome of interest is categorical. While in principle similar to the data types discussed in earlier sections, categorical outcomes pose a challenge because standard scatterplots or correlation measures often are not meaningful. On the other hand, categorical outcomes are becoming more and more prevalent, especially in marketing, where managers are often interested in understanding the choices that consumers make – and choice data is inherently categorical.

Data: Table 2.9 shows credit data for a consumer-to-consumer (C2C) lending market. In this market, consumers ("borrowers") can post loan listings, and other

Table 2.9 Consumer-to-consumer lending data. See also file LoanData.csv.

Status	Credit Grade	Amount	Age	Borrower Rate	Debt-Income Ratio
Current	C	5000	4	0.150	0.040
Default	HR	1900	6	0.265	0.020
Current	HR	1000	3	0.150	0.020
Late	HR	1000	5	0.290	0.020
Current	AA	2550	8	0.079	0.033
Late	NC	1500	2	0.260	0.030
Current	HR	3001	6	0.288	0.020
Current	E	2000	6	0.250	0.020

consumers ("lenders") can invest in those loans by bidding on borrowers' loan rates. The data shows the status of the loan (current, late, and default), the borrower's credit grade (AA is the highest grade, followed by A, B, ..., E; HC stands for "high risk" and denotes the lowest grade; NC stands for "no credit rating"). The data also has information on the amount borrowed (in US$), the age of the loan (in months), the borrower rate (i.e., the interest rate the borrower pays the lender), and the debt-to-income ratio of the borrower.

Goal: The goal is to distinguish good loans from bad. In other words, we want to investigate how a lender can determine which loans will result in timely payments ("Current") and which will result in late payments or even in defaults. Note that the prediction problem is slightly different from all the other examples we have studied before: while previously the goal was to predict the outcome of a numerical variable (e.g., house price, amount spent, or quarterly sales), now we need to predict a categorical variable, "Status." Status assumes the values current, late, or default and is thus not measured on a numerical scale. The problem with predicting categorical variables is that traditional models (which assume numerical variables) do not apply. This is also important for the exploration task since we need to choose our data visualizations carefully, as otherwise we will not get the right answers to our questions.

When visualizing data with categorical outcomes, one typically visualizes the distribution of input variables at all levels of the outcome variable. For instance, in the case of the loan data, we may want to investigate if the distribution of the loan amount differs between loans that are current and those that are late. In fact, if we detected a systematic difference, then this would indicate that the size of the loan amount is a good indicator of future loan performance. Similarly, we may also want to investigate whether the distribution of credit grades differs systematically across different loan statuses because if we found a systematic difference, then the conclusion would again be similar to that above, namely that credit grade is a good predictor of loan performance. Thus, while in both cases we want to investigate the *distribution* of an input (or predictor) variable at all levels of the outcome (or response) variable, the exact way we accomplish this depends on type of input variable. In the following, we discuss two examples, one in which the input variable is numerical and another where the input variable is categorical. To that end, we will use *density plots* and *spine plots*.

Density Plots: A density plot is similar to a histogram. In fact, the only difference between a histogram and a density plot is that while the former selects "buckets" of a certain length and then plots the frequency in each bucket, density plots can be thought of as histograms with arbitrarily small buckets. Thus, their advantage is that they represent the data distribution in the most granular form.

Figure 2.13 shows a density plot for the loan data. In fact, we see density plots for each of the four numerical variables: amount borrowed, age of loan, borrower rate, and debt-to-income ratio. Moreover, for each variable, the density is broken up by the status of the loan: the black lines correspond to densities of current loans; the green lines correspond to late loans; and the red lines correspond to loans in default. We can see that while the distribution of loan amount (top left panel) is almost identical across all three loan statuses, it is very different for the age of the loan (top right panel). In fact, the graph suggests that many current loans are young (i.e., only a few months of age), while most defaulted loans are old (i.e., five or more months old). While this result is not completely surprising (a consumer typically defaults after a certain period of time and not immediately after taking out the loan), it does suggest a way to distinguish between good and bad loans. Figure 2.13 suggests additional ways in which loans can be distinguished. The bottom left panel

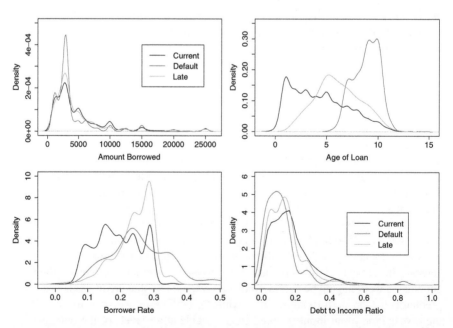

Fig. 2.13 Distribution of amount borrowed, age of loan, borrower rate, and debt-to-income ratio, broken up by different loan outcomes (current, late, or default).

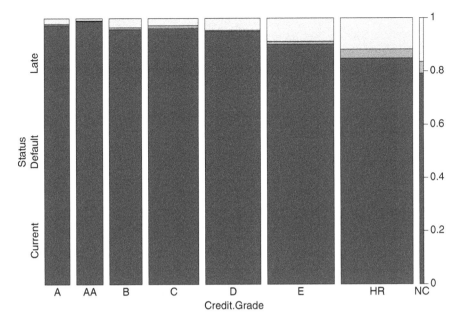

Fig. 2.14 Credit grade by loan outcome.

(borrower rate) suggests that late or defaulting loans have higher loan rates; the bottom right panel also suggest that a low debt-to-income ratio does not necessarily signal a good loan.

Spine Plots: Spine plots are a way of visualizing cross-tabulations (e.g., relationships between two categorical variables). Figure 2.14 shows a spine plot between the loan status and the credit grade. Black bars correspond to current loans, dark grey bars correspond to loans in default, and light grey bars correspond to loans that are late. The width of the bar corresponds to the number of loans with a particular credit grade. (For instance, the "A" bar is thinner than the "C" bar, suggesting that there are many more loans graded C than A.)

We can learn that, unsurprisingly, as the grade deteriorates, the number of late and defaulted loans increases. In particular, HR (high-risk) loans have the greatest number of loans in default or that are late. It is interesting to note, though, that while there are only a small number of nongraded loans (NC), their default and late-payment rates are is even higher than for high-risk loans. Thus, credit grade is a very strong predictor of loan status.

Lessons Learned:

- Density plots and spine plots are very powerful tools for investigating data where the response is categorical. The main idea of these plots is to split up one of the input variables (e.g., age of the loan) by the different levels of the target variable. For instance, we could plot histograms for different levels of loan status or, as in the case of density plots, create histograms of extremely fine granularity.

- Categorical responses occur frequently in business data, especially in marketing, where we study customers' choices and preferences. While traditional scatterplots are not very useful for exploring data with categorical responses, density plots and spine plots can unveil new, previously unknown knowledge.

2.6   Graphs for Panel Data: Customer Loyalty Data

We finish this chapter by giving a glimpse into yet another challenging form of business data: panel data. Panel data occurs when we follow a set of customers over time and record their behavior and preferences. Thus, panel data share similarities with time series data (for each panel member, we have a time series of observations); on the other hand, panel data also has cross-sectional features, as the panel contains a sample of different customers. Understanding all the information that panel data carries is not easy, and we want to explain the challenges in the following section.

Data: Table 2.10 shows purchasing data for nine randomly selected customers of an Internet DVD rental business for a period of 12 months (January–December). Each of the 12 columns refers to the amount of money a customer spends in a given month. For instance, customer 2 spends $114.33 in the month of February and continues to spend rather frequently until the end of September (after which he makes no further purchases). On the other hand, customer 1 made a single purchase ($25.74) that occurred in February, and she did not spend any more money in subsequent months. We also see that some customers spend nothing at all during the entire year (e.g., customers 6, 7, and 9).

Table 2.10 Customer loyalty data. See also file `CustomerLoyalty.csv`.

ID	Jan	Feb	Mar	Apr	May	Jun	Jul	Aug	Sep	Oct	Nov	Dec
1	0	25.74	0	0	0	0	0	0	0	0	0	0
2	0	114.33	108.56	51.28	0	52.28	70.07	40.1	47.96	0	0	0
3	21.54	0	0	0	0	0	0	0	0	0	0	0
4	0	0	0	0	0	0	0	0	0	0	0	0
5	0	8.79	42.1	0	0	10.77	63.25	27.93	0	63.45	83.94	30.98
6	0	0	0	0	0	0	0	0	0	0	0	0
7	0	0	0	0	0	0	0	0	0	0	0	0
8	0	24.48	13.97	0	48.37	0	52.27	0	0	0	0	0
9	0	0	0	0	0	0	0	0	0	0	0	0

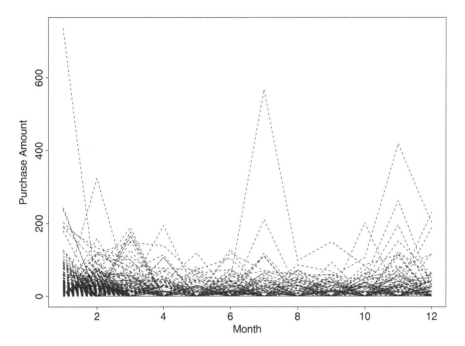

Fig. 2.15   Time series plots for all customers in the panel.

Goal: The goal of the analysis is to understand purchasing patterns. Why do some customers spend more money than others? And when do they spend their money (early in the year or towards the end of the year)? And why do some customers make only one-time purchases while others spend frequently? Can we segment customers by their purchasing patterns? Answers to some of these questions could help our business target individual customers with tailored coupons and promotions. For instance, customers who only spend at the beginning of the year could be enticed to spend additional money in later months via coupons that are valid only for the holidays. On the other hand, if we knew that a customer only made one-time purchases and if we knew the timing of that purchase, then we could maximize that single purchase with the right advertising and promotions offered at the right time.

Overlaid Time Series Plots: We introduced time series plots in Section 2.3. We have also argued above that panel data are essentially a bunch of individual time series – one series for each customer. So, why not plot all those time series (one per customer) into one single graph, you may ask? Well, the answer is that this kind of approach often leads to information overload and clutter; that is, our attempt at exploring all the available data at once leads to more information than the graph can carry and, as a result, we don't learn much at all!

Take as an example Figure 2.15, which shows the purchase pattern for all customers, across all months, in one graph. We refer to this graph as an *overlaid time series plot* since we essentially took many individual time series and overlaid them all together on one page. Note that we attempted to make the graph as clean as possible by choosing dashed lines, which results in as little clutter as possible.

All in all, we cannot learn much from Figure 2.15. We can learn that there exist some (in fact, rather few) customers who make remarkably large purchases at select instances throughout the year. (Notice the high spikes at the beginning and at the end of the year, and also the unusually high spike at month 7.) However, while these few customers bring exceptional value to our business at select occasions, they are not representative of the *typical* customer. The typical customer is "hidden" in the line clutter at the bottom of the graph.

The main problem with Figure 2.15 is that it tries to accomplish too much: it tries to represent both the temporal information (i.e., the purchasing pattern of each customer over time) and the cross-sectional information (i.e., the variation across customers). While preserving as much information about the data as possible is often a very valuable objective, this is an example where data aggregation will lead to better insight. What we mean by that is that we should first try to aggregate the data (either by its temporal or cross-sectional component) and only then graph it. In the following, we discuss several ways of accomplishing this aggregation task. It is important to note that the actual graphs that we use are standard and have been introduced in earlier sections (e.g., histograms); however, we apply these graphs in an innovative way to take advantage of the special structure of panel data.

Aggregating the Cross-sectional Dimension: Panel data have two main dimensions: temporal information and cross-sectional information. If we want to explore trends over time, then we should aggregate over the cross-sectional dimension and keep the temporal dimension intact. Aggregation can be done in a variety of ways. For instance, we could – for each month of the year – compute the average purchase amount; that is, we could compute numerical summary statistics for each month of the year. Alternatively, we could visualize the purchase distribution in each month using month-by-month histograms. This is shown in Figure 2.16.

Figure 2.16 shows that purchasing patterns differ from month to month. While January features a large number of high-value purchases (i.e., purchases with amounts up to $20 or $40), purchase amounts decline in subsequent months. In fact, January, February, July, and November appear to be the months in which a customer spends the most money during a single visit.

While the amount a customer spends matters, it equally matters whether a customer spends anything at all. In fact, Figure 2.16 does not quite tell us what proportion of our customers made any purchase at all. To that end, we can employ a similar rationale as above and compute month-by-month pie charts (see Figure 2.17). Note that each pie chart compares the proportion of customers who did not make any purchase (denoted by "0" and colored in white) with those who made a purchase (denoted by "1" and colored black).

We can learn that January, February, March, and maybe June are the months in which most customers make a purchase. In fact, as pointed out above, January and

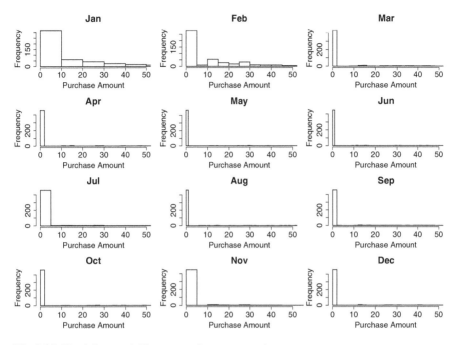

Fig. 2.16   Month-by-month histograms of customer purchases.

February are also the months in which a customer spends the most money during a single visit. Hence, these two months appear to be our most profitable month. The month of March is interesting because it is marked by many visits but relatively low spending per visit. On the other hand, while the month of July does not see a high number of visits, the amount spent per visit is rather high.

All in all, the aggregation of our panel data has led to new insight regarding the timing and amount of purchase decisions. While some months see more frequent customer visits (but are marked by lower purchase amounts), other months see higher purchase amounts (but less frequently). This insight could lead our marketing department to devise seasonally varying advertising and promotion strategies that during some periods aim at increasing the amount a customer spends ("budget focus") and during other periods aim at increasing a customer's purchase frequency ("frequency focus").

Aggregating the Temporal Dimension: Instead of aggregating over the cross-sectional information, we could also aggregate over the temporal information (and hence keep the cross-sectional information intact). In our situation, the cross-sectional information corresponds to the variation from one customer to another. Figure 2.18 shows customer-specific histograms (for the first 25 customers in our data). Each histogram shows the distribution of purchases made by this customer over the period of one year. In other words, while Figure 2.18 pre-

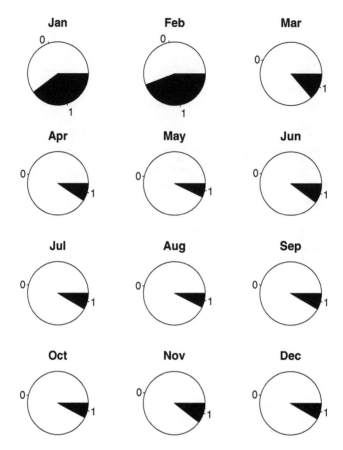

Fig. 2.17 Month-by-month pie charts of customer purchases.

serves the customer-to-customer differences, it loses the temporal information: we are no longer able to determine whether customer 1 made the purchase of $25 in January or in July. This is what we mean by aggregating over temporal information.

The usefulness of Figure 2.18 is limited and depends on our objective. If our goal is to develop customer-specific spending patterns, then Figure 2.18 tells us that, for example, customer 5 has a very different pattern compared with customers 6 and 13. However, recall that Figure 2.18 shows only a snapshot of the first 25 customers – if our panel contains several thousand (or even million) customers, then this approach would be quite cumbersome. Moreover, since we plot different histograms for different customers, we don't quite learn what is *common* across customers. In other words, panel data are challenging and one has to think very carefully about how best to extract the kind of knowledge that supports one's business goals.

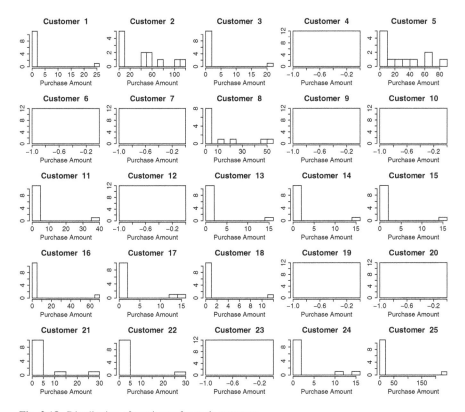

Fig. 2.18   Distribution of purchases for each customer.

Lessons Learned:

- Data aggregation is often useful prior to exploring panel data; data can be aggregated with respect to either temporal dimension or cross-sectional dimension.
- Sequences of histograms, pie charts, boxplots, or any other form of numerical or graphical summary can be useful for exploring aggregated panel data.

Chapter 3
Data Modeling I – Basics

In this chapter, we introduce methods for modeling data. We refer to these methods as "basics" since they form the foundation for many of the more advanced ideas and concepts discussed in later chapters. The most basic concept is that of a model itself. You may ask: "What is a model? And why do we need models at all?" We will give answers to these fundamental questions in Section 3.1. In Section 3.2, we will discuss linear regression models as one of the most widespread and versatile types of models. The name "linear" implies that we will discuss models that assume that the relationship follows a straight line. For instance, you may argue that the more you eat, the more weight you gain – and you may gain an additional pound of body weight for every pound of food that you eat. That's exactly what we mean by a linear model: every unit of "input" has the same (proportional) impact on the "output." If I eat 2 pounds of food, I will gain 2 pounds in body weight; and if I eat 4 pounds, I will gain 4 pounds of body weight, and so on – the relationship between input and output is always the same (1 to 1 in this case). You will quickly realize that while the concept of linear models is extremely powerful, it also has its limitations. For instance, do you really believe that the entire world follows linear relationships? If, for instance, human growth was linear and increased by the same rate every year, why is it that by the time we reach the age of 50, we are not 50 feet tall? In that sense, we will also discuss limitations of linear regression throughout this chapter. Some of these limitations will be addressed immediately, while others will be our motivation for more advanced methods discussed in subsequent chapters.

In Section 3.2, we will show how to apply linear regression to a set of data and – most importantly – we will show how to read and interpret the results. In fact, much of this book focuses on understanding the results from regression and other types of models and methods. While it is often quite easy to *compute* a regression model – often, it takes no more than the click of a mouse – the real challenge lies in understanding the results and deriving business knowledge from them. This will be our main focus in Section 3.2. Section 3.3 focuses on another important aspect of modeling: distinguishing the important pieces of information from the not-so-important ones. In fact, most modeling algorithms are rather "brainless" and do exactly what you tell them to do. If you tell the algorithm to incorporate a certain

W. Jank, *Business Analytics for Managers*, Use R!, DOI 10.1007/978-1-4614-0406-4_3,   41
© Springer Science+Business Media, LLC 2011

piece of information, then it will readily do so. So the burden is on you to weed out the good information from what is not so relevant. To that end, there exist a variety of statistical tools, often referred to as "statistical inference," that can help with the weeding-out process. Statistical inference tries to establish the signal that resides in the data and contrasts it against the noise – and if the signal-to-noise ratio is not large, then inferential methods will typically suggest that a certain piece of information is not too relevant for our cause and should be dropped.

3.1   Introduction: Why Do We Need Models?

We start out by discussing the basic ideas and concepts of a model. You may ask "What is a model?" and "Why do we need models altogether?" The answer is that models are typically thought of as an abstraction of (or an approximation to) reality. And we often need them because we have a deep desire to understand the past, learn from it, and then predict the future. This desire is especially prevalent in business, where we would like to know answers to questions such as "How many customers will visit my store tomorrow?", "Should I manufacture 1,000 or 10,000 smart phones?", or "If I invest my money in stock A today, will its value go up tomorrow?"

Many business decisions are driven by our ability to anticipate the future. In fact, the difference between a successful business venture and a failure often hinges on our ability to predict the future, to anticipate our customer's behavior or our competitors' moves. Models play a key part in this process. Models allow us to separate data into predictable and unpredictable elements. In fact, models separate (unpredictable) noise from (predictable) patterns. By learning from patterns that occurred in the past (and maybe adjusting or updating these patterns according to present events), we are often able to predict the future.

To make the discussion more concrete, let's consider the following (purposefully simple) example. Table 3.1 shows information on sales of a particular type of soft drink distributed across different sales regions. In addition to sales information, the table also records the amount of money spent on advertising in each region.

Table 3.1 The sales and advertising data. Data are recorded in thousands of dollars. See also file `Sales&Advertising.csv`.

Sales	Advt
145.1	9.5
128.3	10.1
121.3	9.4
134.4	11.6
106.5	10.3
111.5	9.5
132.7	11.2
126.9	9
151	11

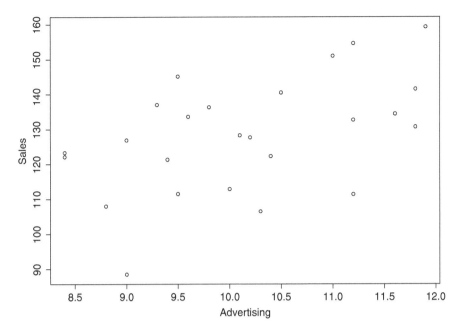

Fig. 3.1 Scatterplot between advertising and sales for the soft drink data.

Who would be interested in this kind of data, and how would they want to use it? Well, the marketing manager for one, because the data may (or may not!) show that the efforts that she and her team spend on advertising truly matter. In other words, the marketing manager may have a hunch that there is a positive relationship between advertising and sales (i.e., the more money spent on advertising, the more sales grow). But how can she support this hunch? We have already learned some basic tools in Chapter 2: the simplest (and at the same time most powerful) tool to support this hunch would be to create a *scatterplot* between advertising and sales. Figure 3.1 shows this scatterplot.

What can we learn from Figure 3.1? Well, we can learn that there exists a *positive relationship* between advertising and sales (i.e., sales generally increase as advertising increases), and hence the manager's hunch proves correct. But is this really all that we are interested in? Consider the company's CEO, who asks the marketing manager the following question:

"Are your advertising efforts effective?"

What does the CEO mean by "effective"? One way to interpret "effective" would be by asking the question somewhat differently: "Is there enough bang for the buck?" Or, phrased in more formal language: "For every dollar we spend on advertising, do we get enough in return (via sales)?" For instance, what if for every dollar we spend on advertising we only get a 10 cent return on sales? Would you be happy with that? Would your CEO be happy with that? On the other hand, what if for every dollar you invest in advertising, sales return, on average, $10? Wouldn't that make you (and your team) much happier? But how can we *quantify* the impact of our advertising efforts? Can we quantify it from Figure 3.1? The simple answer is "No"! We cannot quantify patterns that we only "see" in a graph. In order to quantify a relationship, we need a model!

So, what is a model? A model – in its simplest form – is a mathematical equation. In the previous example, a (hypothetical) model could look like the following equation:

$$\text{Sales} = \$10{,}000 + 5 \times \text{Advertising} \tag{3.1}$$

What does this equation mean? First, we can use it to estimate different levels of sales for different levels of advertising spending. For instance, assume we spend $20,000 on advertising. How large do you expect sales to be (using the model above)? The answer is, simply "plug in" Advertising = $20,000 on the right-hand side of equation (3.1), and we get

$$\text{Sales} = \$10{,}000 + (5) \times (\$20{,}000)$$

which equals $110,000. In other words, the model tells us that when we spend $20,000 on advertising, we expect to see roughly $110,000 in sales. The quality of this prediction depends on the quality of our model: better models will result in predictions that are closer to the truth!

In this context, it would be wise to caution the reader early on about the use (and misuse) of models. While models are powerful and can be an enormous help for prediction and planning purposes, they are only as good as we make them! That is, if we don't spend much effort looking for the best possible model, then we can't expect much from them. In the same vein, models are only as good as the data we "feed" into them: poor data on the input side will result in poor predictions on the output side. We will see many examples of this data quality issue throughout this book. And one last comment: a famous statistician once said that "all models are wrong, only some are better than others."[1] This implies that we should not rely exclusively on a model – common sense and business experience are equally important for making good decisions!

Let's come back to our model in equation (3.1). What else can we learn from the following relationship?

$$\text{Sales} = \$10{,}000 + 5 \times \text{Advertising}$$

In particular, what does the number "$10,000" tells us? Think about it in the following way: If we did not spend any money at all on advertising, would we still sell our product? Likely! How much would we sell? As per our model, we would sell

$$\text{Sales} = \$10{,}000 + (5) \times (\$0)$$

---

[1] These words are usually attributed to the famous statistician George Box.

(Note that since we do not spend any money on advertising, we set Advertising = $0 in our model.) The result is $10,000. So $10,000 denotes the amount of sales in the absence of any advertising.

Furthermore, how can we interpret the number "5" in our model? Not sure? Then let's consider the following scenario: Let's consider two marketing managers. One manager proposes to spend $10,000 on advertising; the other one proposes to spend $11,000 on advertising. What are the expected sales for managers 1 and 2? They are, respectively,

$$\text{Sales} = \$10,000 + (5) \times (\$10,000) = \$60,000$$

for manager 1 and

$$\text{Sales} = \$10,000 + (5) \times (\$11,000) = \$65,000$$

for manager 2. So what is the difference between managers 1 and 2? It is

$$\$65,000 - \$60,000 = \$5,000$$

In other words, since manager 2 spends $1,000 *more* on advertising, he gets $5,000 *more* in sales returns. Or, put differently one more time, for every additional dollar he spends, he gets five additional dollars in return. That's exactly the meaning of the value "5" in our model – it measures how *fast* sales increase for each additional dollar we spend on advertising. We also refer to this value as the *slope* of the model; in a similar vein, the value $10,000 is also referred to as the *intercept*, as it indicates where the model "intercepts" the Y-axis (i.e., the value where the response – sales in our case – equals zero).

Not convinced yet? How about the following (different) model?

$$\text{Sales} = \$10,000 + 2 \times \text{Advertising}$$

Compared with model (3.1) above, do sales now increase faster or slower for each additional dollar we spend on advertising?[2]

Another illustration of model (3.1) is shown in the left panel of Figure 3.2. Here, we see values of sales plotted against a range of different values of advertising. The blue triangle illustrates the meaning of the slope. If we increased advertising from $10,000 to $30,000, then we would "walk" 20,000 units to the right along the advertising axis. This is illustrated by the horizontal part of the triangle. The increase in advertising would result in a de facto gain in "altitude" by 100,000 units (illustrated by the vertical part of the triangle); in other words, sales would increase

---

[2]The answer is: Sales now increase at a slower rate. In fact, now, for each additional advertising dollar, sales only increase by two dollars. Compare this to an increase of five dollars in the previous model.

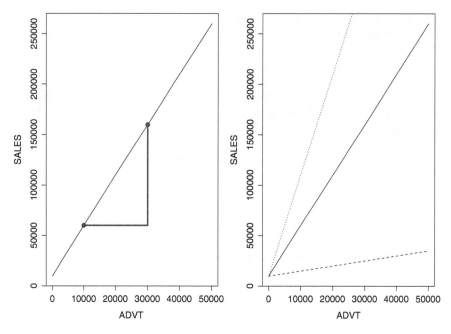

Fig. 3.2 Left panel: A graphical illustration of the model in (3.1). Right panel: Alternative models with slopes of 0.5 and 10, respectively.

by $100,000. The right panel of Figure 3.2 shows two additional models, one with a slope of 0.5 (dashed line) and the other with a slope of 10 (dotted line). We can see that the magnitude of the slope directly translates into the "steepness" of the line: While the line corresponding to a slope of 0.5 (bottom line) is rather flat, a slope of 10 results in a very steep slope.

Lessons Learned:

- We have discussed the importance of mathematical models for decision making. Models are an abstraction of reality, and they separate predictable patterns from unpredictable noise. Models are important because they allow us to quantify a relationship: while scatterplots and correlation tables will tell us about the qualitative nature of a relationship (e.g., positive vs. negative, weak vs. strong), they do not tell us exactly how the output changes as a result of changes to the input variables. In other words, models allow us to quantify precisely how much we expect sales to grow for each additional amount of spending on advertising for example. Without a model, we could not forecast the future and, as a result, could not conduct meaningful planning.

- We have also discussed the difference between the slope and the intercept of a model and their practical interpretations. The intercept denotes the part of the model where the line intersects the Y-axis. The importance of this number is that it denotes the amount of output in the absence of any input (e.g., the amount of sales without any advertising). The slope, on the other hand, tells us how fast the output will grow for each additional unit of the input variables. For instance, it could tell us that sales will grow by an additional \$5 for each \$1 increase in advertising. The slope of a model is particularly important because it allows us to gauge the statistical and practical importance of an input variable. In the following, much emphasis will be placed on interpreting the slope correctly.

3.2 Fitting and Interpreting a Regression Model: Least Squares Regression

In this section, we will discuss two related questions:

1. How can we *obtain* a model such as the one in equation (3.1)?
2. And, more importantly, how can we *interpret* such a model and use it for business insight?

When we say "obtain a model," we really mean "use data to obtain a model." All of this book focuses on deriving business insight from data. Clearly, there are many ways of obtaining a model such as in equation (3.1) *without* the use of any data. For instance, one could ask several experts about their best guess at the relationship in equation (3.1). While these kinds of "brainstorming sessions" are (unfortunately) rather common business practice, this is not what we have in mind here. Our goal is to derive a model based purely on objective, data-driven facts rather than relying on gut feeling and guesswork. This is not to say that a manager's experience plays no role in data-driven decision making. On the contrary, a manager's experience can be extremely valuable when used in *conjunction* with data-driven models and methods. In fact, experience plays a particularly important role when interpreting and applying the results from data-driven models. We will see examples very soon.

We also pointed out above that we will put more emphasis on the *interpretation* of models rather than on their estimation. The reason is that one can often estimate a model with the click of a mouse. However, what is typically much harder is to understand the results and to use them for decision making. In that sense, we will not cover all of those mathematical and statistical details that one typically encounters in a traditional statistics textbook. Rather, we will give a verbal explanation of some of the conceptual and methodological underpinnings and then quickly move on to applying and interpreting the methods. We will start out by discussing the most common, well-known, and powerful method of obtaining a model, which is often referred to as the *least squares regression* method.

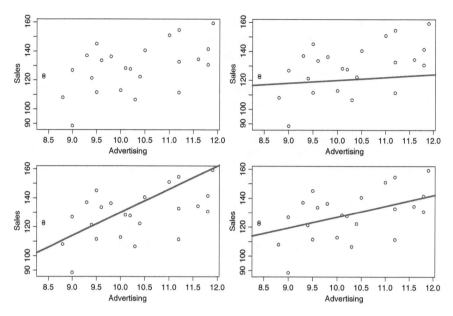

Fig. 3.3   Soft drink sales data from Table 3.1 and three potential models for that data.

3.2.1   The Idea of Least Squares Regression

Consider the scatterplot from Figure 3.1, which is reproduced in the top left panel of
Figure 3.3. When we talk about "obtaining a model," we mean a process that leads
us from the data in this scatterplot to a model such as in equation (3.1). How can
we find such a model? And how can we find the *best possible* model? For instance,
which of the three lines in Figure 3.3 constitutes the best model for our data? The
line in the top right panel appears too flat; on the other hand, the trend in the data
does not appear to be growing as fast as the line in the bottom left panel. So, does
the line in the bottom right panel correspond to the best possible model? Visually,
this line appears to capture the trend in the data very well. But should we trust our
eyes? And, can we quantify *how well* that line fits the data? To that end, we use a
method that is referred to as *least squares regression.*

Least squares regression finds the best (or optimal) model by minimizing the
sum of the squared residuals. It is important to realize that this is just one way
of defining "the best" model; another way would be to minimize the *sum of the
absolute residuals,* and there are even other criteria. Consider Figure 3.4. It shows
four sample data points (given by the four solid dots) and a hypothetical line through
that data. We want to use that figure to illustrate the concept of least squares
regression.

Clearly, we can find many different lines through these four data points. But how
can we quantify which line best resembles the trend in the data? To that end, let's

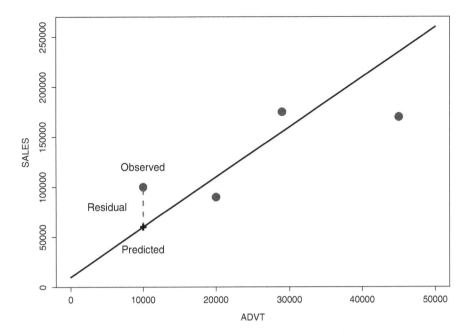

Fig. 3.4 Illustration of observed, predicted, and residual values.

refer to the actual data as the *observed* data point. Also, if we consider the projection of the observed data onto the line (indicated by the dotted lines), then we refer to the corresponding points on the line as the *predicted* values. The difference between the observed and the predicted values measures how well our model fits the data; smaller differences imply a better fit. This difference (which is given by the length of the dotted lines) is also referred to as the *residual*. Since we have many different data points, we have many different residual values. Least squares regression determines the best model by finding the line that *minimizes the sum of all squared residuals.*

A few more comments on this process are in order. Why do we square the residuals? Because we feel that large negative residuals (i.e., points far below the line) are as bad as large positive ones (i.e., points that are high above the line). By squaring the residual values, we treat positive and negative discrepancies in the same way.[3] And why do we sum all the squared residuals? Because we cannot

---

[3]Rather than squaring residuals, we could also take their absolute values. Both approaches have the effect that negative discrepancies are considered as bad as positive ones. So why do we square rather than take absolute values? The answer probably depends on who you ask. One answer is grounded in history. Least squares regression goes back to the famous mathematician Carl Friedrich Gauss in the eighteenth century. Back in the eighteenth century, computers were not available. So, in order to compute a regression line, one would have to do the calculations by hand. We can determine the minimum of the sum of the squared residuals manually because it only involves minimizing a quadratic function, which can be done by taking the first derivative.

find a single straight line that minimizes all residuals simultaneously. Instead, we minimize the *average* (squared) residual value. In fact, minimizing the average has the same result as minimizing the sum (since the only difference between the average and the sum is the normalizing constant $\frac{1}{n}$). In other words, least squares regression finds that line (among all possible lines) that results in the smallest average squared residual distance.

3.2.2 Interpreting a First Simple Regression Model

Let's see an example. Consider again the data from Table 3.1 shown in Figure 3.1. We have available two pieces of information, advertising and sales, and we have argued earlier that we would be interested in understanding if (and how) advertising affects sales. To that end, we would like to estimate a model of the form

$$\text{Sales} = a + b \times \text{Advertising} \tag{3.2}$$

Note that this is the same model as in equation (3.1) except that we have now replaced the numbers 10,000 and 5 by generic placeholders a and b, respectively. Note that we typically refer to such placeholders as *coefficients*. Also note that in equation (3.1) we had just made up the numbers 10,000 and 5 – now, we want to *estimate* the true numbers from the data. To that end, we use least squares regression.

Least squares estimation is typically performed with a simple click of the mouse or by typing a single line of code into software. That is not the challenge. The challenge typically lies in interpreting the output. The software output corresponding to the least squares regression estimation of model (3.2) is shown in Figure 3.5. We can see that a simple click of the mouse (or a single line of code) has triggered quite a lot of information. We now discuss how to interpret all of this information.

Least squares estimation triggers a *lot* of output, often more than can be digested easily. For that reason, we will – at least for now – only focus on the two pieces of information highlighted by the two boxes in Figure 3.5. First, we will focus on the information presented in the first box (labeled "Part I" in Figure 3.5). Then, we will focus on the box below (labeled "Part II"). While the remaining information is not unimportant, it is not directly necessary for the purpose of interpreting our least squares regression model.

Consider the information given in the first box of Figure 3.5 ("Part I"). We can see two rows (marked as "(Intercept)" and "ADVT") and four columns. For now, let's only focus on the first column. The first column shows the estimates for the coefficients of the model in equation (3.2). These estimates are 51.849 and 7.527,

---

In contrast, minimizing a function that involves absolute values is much more involved and requires iterative (i.e., computer-driven) calculations.

```
Call:
lm(formula = SALES ~ ADVT)

Residuals:
     Min        1Q    Median        3Q       Max
 -31.0945   -9.9708   0.4255    9.6146   21.7419
```

Part I

```
Coefficients:
              Estimate Std. Error t value Pr(>|t|)
(Intercept)     51.849     27.990   1.852   0.0768 .
ADVT             7.527      2.741   2.746   0.0115 *
---
```

Signif. codes: 0 '***' 0.001 '**' 0.01 '*' 0.05 '.' 0.1 ' ' 1

```
Residual standard error: 14.51 on 23 degrees of freedom
Multiple R-squared: 0.2469,      Adjusted R-squared: 0.2142
F-statistic:  7.54 on 1 and 23 DF,  p-value: 0.01151
```

Part II

Fig. 3.5 Software output for a first simple regression model.

respectively. In fact, 51.849 is the estimate for the coefficient a, and 7.527 is the estimate for the coefficient b. Together, this leads to the *estimated* model

$$\text{Sales} = 51.849 + 7.527 \times \text{Advertising} \qquad (3.3)$$

Applying the concepts learned in Section 3.1, we already know how to interpret this model.

Interpreting the intercept a = 51.849: Equation (3.3) shows that the estimate for the coefficient a equals 51.849. Recall that we also refer to this coefficient as the *intercept* of the regression line (i.e., the point where the regression line in Figure 3.6 intercepts the Y-axis). What does this value mean? It means that 51.849 equals the amount of sales with zero advertising. In other words, in the absence of any advertising expenditures, we can still expect a sales volume of $51.849 on average.[4] This makes sense since marketing is not the only driver of sales. In fact, this is an example where the interpretation of the intercept makes conceptual sense. We will see examples in the future where the intercept will not always have a meaningful interpretation.

Interpreting the Slope b = 7.527: Equation (3.3) also shows that the estimate for the coefficient b equals 7.527. We have argued earlier that b is the *slope* of the regression in Figure 3.6. Thus, $b = 7.527$ implies that for every $1 *increase* in

---

[4]Note that both sales and advertising are recorded in thousands of dollars, so the more accurate interpretation of the value of a is that, in the absence of any advertising, the company still records sales of $51,849 on average.

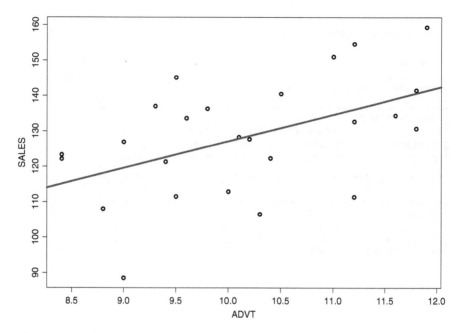

Fig. 3.6 Regression line for the estimated regression model in Figure 3.5.

advertising sales increase by $7.527.[5] Thus, every dollar spent on advertising has more than a sevenfold effect on sales – which should make the marketing manager rather happy!

3.2.3   Evaluating a Regression Model

We now move on to interpreting the information in the second box of Figure 3.5 (marked as "Part II"). In particular, we will initially focus exclusively on interpreting the "multiple R-squared" value. Multiple R-squared is for simplicity often referred to as "R-squared" or R^2.

R-squared measures the overall quality of a regression model. By "quality" we mean a measure of how well the (idealized) model tracks the (actual) data. Consider Figure 3.7 for an illustration of the concept of R-squared.

---

[5]Similar to the previous footnote, we remind the reader that since both data are recorded in thousands of dollars, the more appropriate interpretation would be "for every increase in advertising by $1,000, sales increase by $7,527," which reflects the scaling of the recorded data.

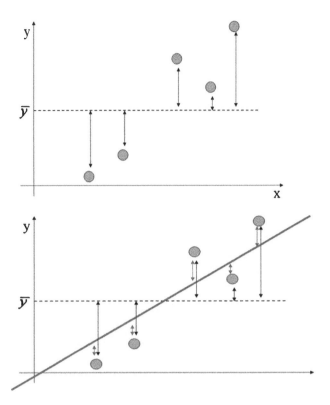

Fig. 3.7   Illustration of R-squared.

The top panel in Figure 3.7 shows five hypothetical data points (indicated by the filled circles). Let's assume for the moment that we only know the information on the Y-axis and that we do not have any information available on the X-axis. (In other words, we only have available information about sales, not about advertising expenditures.) For that situation, what would be our best "model"? Well, since we only have information about sales, our best model would be given by the *average* of sales, or $\bar{y}$, which is indicated by the dotted line. However, sales vary across different sales regions, so how good is that model? One way to assess the quality of that model is via its *variance*: the arrows between the data points and dotted line measure the deviation of each individual sales region and the overall model; larger deviations indicate sales regions where the model provides a poorer fit. Squaring all deviations and summing the squared deviations leads to the concept of the *total sum of squares* (SST):

$$SST = \sum_{i=1}^{n} (y_i - \bar{y})^2 \tag{3.4}$$

SST is related to the concept of the *sample variance*[6] and measures the *overall variability in the data*. What is variability? Variability is often referred to as *uncertainty*: the more variability there is among sales regions, the higher our uncertainty about the exact performance of any one sales region in particular. In that sense, SST measures the overall variability or uncertainty in our data. The higher the variability, the harder our modeling problem. We take SST as a *benchmark* for our modeling efforts.

Next, consider the bottom panel in Figure 3.7, which shows the effect of estimating a regression model on our data (indicated by the diagonal line). How much of the total uncertainty (SST) has the regression line managed to "model away"? To that end, consider the deviations between the regression line and the data points (indicated by the second set of arrows). We can see that the deviations have generally decreased, which implies that the regression model provides a better fit to the data than our previous average-sales model. But there is still some uncertainty left, even after applying the regression model. How much is left? We can again sum all squared deviations, which leads to the concept of the *error sum of squares* (SSE):

$$SSE = \sum_{i=1}^{n} (y_i - \hat{y}_i)^2 \tag{3.5}$$

SSE measures how much variability (or uncertainty) there is left in the data after applying the regression model. We can combine the concepts of overall uncertainty (SST) and uncertainty left over after applying the regression model (SSE) to come up with a measure for how much the model has helped reduce the uncertainty:

$$SSR = SST - SSE \tag{3.6}$$

This quantifies the uncertainty that the regression model was able to model away. Thus, the *proportion* of the total variability that the regression was able to capture is referred to as *R-squared*, and it is given by

$$R\text{-squared} = \frac{SSR}{SST} \tag{3.7}$$

Interpreting *R*-squared $= 0.2469$: Coming back to the *R*-squared value of 0.2469 in Figure 3.5, we can now conclude that our regression model explains 24.69% of the total variability in sales. Is this good or bad? Well, it depends. In fact, the perceived quality of *R*-squared depends on the context. Chemists performing lab experiments would probably perceive an *R*-squared value of 24.69% as outrageously poor; the reason is that in lab experiments one can often control almost all extraneous factors. On the other hand, social scientists (or business executives, for that matter) often feel that a 24.69% *R*-squared is reasonably high, because it is

---

[6]In fact, if we divide SST by $(n-1)$, we obtain the sample variance.

```
Call:
lm(formula = SALES ~ ADVT + INCOME)

Residuals:
      Min        1Q    Median        3Q       Max
  -22.6876   -6.0687    0.6043    7.0523   28.5334

Coefficients:
               Estimate Std. Error t value Pr(>|t|)
(Intercept)     36.8948    24.9629   1.478   0.1536
ADVT             5.0691     2.5397   1.996   0.0585 .
INCOME           0.8081     0.2816   2.870   0.0089 **
---
Signif. codes:  0 '***' 0.001 '**' 0.01 '*' 0.05 '.' 0.1 ' ' 1

Residual standard error: 12.66 on 22 degrees of freedom
Multiple R-squared: 0.452,      Adjusted R-squared: 0.4022
F-statistic: 9.074 on 2 and 22 DF,  p-value: 0.001338
```

Fig. 3.8 Software output for a regression model on advertising and median household income.

typically very hard to control extraneous factors when dealing with humans (such as customers or suppliers). So, the magnitude of R-squared has to be evaluated in context, and there is no single benchmark that applies equally to all situations. However, one suitable use of R-squared is to compare two (or more) competing regression models with one another. We will describe this application next.

3.2.4 Comparing Regression Models

Consider Figure 3.8, which shows the software output for another regression model. In fact, the only difference compared with the previous model is that we added a second explanatory variable, "INCOME," which denotes the median household income in each sales region. Thus, the formal model is now

$$\text{Sales} = a + b_1 \times \text{Advertising} + b_2 \times \text{Income} \qquad (3.8)$$

Glancing over the output in Figure 3.8, we can quickly identify that the estimated coefficients for a, b_1, and b_2 are now

$a = 36.8949$
$b_1 = 5.0691$
$b_2 = 0.8081$

However, which model is better, the earlier one in Figure 3.5 or the later one in Figure 3.8? In order to answer that question, let's compare their corresponding R-squared values.

Comparing R-squared Values: The R-squared value for the model in Figure 3.5 equals 24.69%, and that for the model in Figure 3.8 equals 45.20% – clearly, the second model explains a larger proportion of the total uncertainty in sales and is thus a better model. So, we can use R-squared to compare one model with another one. However, some caution is necessary: R-squared has the unpleasant property that it will never decrease, even if we add variables to the model that are complete nonsense. In fact, we could have added the weight of each region's sales manager to the model and R-squared would not have decreased! Thus, we should not overly rely on R-squared alone when comparing models. A related measure (one that *can* increase and decrease) is called *adjusted R-squared*. Adjusted R-squared penalizes the model for the inclusion of nonsense variables, and hence we can use it to compare models with different variables. Let's take a look back at the two models in Figures 3.5 and 3.8. For the first model, the adjusted R-squared equals 0.2142, while it equals 0.4022 for the second one. Thus, since the adjusted R-squared is higher for the second model, we can conclude that it provides a better representation of our data. In other words, the second model wins!

Lessons Learned:

- We estimate models from data using the concepts of least squares regression; least squares finds a regression line that has the shortest average distance to all data points. In that sense, the least squares regression model is optimal in that it best fits the data, at least on average.
- The estimated coefficients (in particular, the intercept and the slope) of the regression line play an important part in interpreting a regression model. While the intercept tells us about the magnitude of the response in the absence of any input, the slope tells us about how fast the response grows for each additional unit of the input variables.
- We can evaluate the quality of a regression model using the concept of R-squared; R-squared measures the percentage of the total uncertainty in the data that is explained by the regression line. Higher values of R-squared denote better models. In fact, we can compare models with one another using the concept of R-squared. However, caution is necessary since R-squared does not penalize the inclusion of nonsense and meaningless variables.
- A better way of comparing regression models is via the so-called adjusted R-squared. Adjusted R-squared penalizes a model for variables that make no sense and have no effect on the output.

3.3   Identifying and Selecting Important Predictors: Statistical Inference

In the previous section, we learned how to estimate a model from data. In fact, applying the concepts from that section, we can estimate *any* model from a given set of data. For instance, Figure 3.5 displays a model with only one predictor, "Advertising." On the other hand, Figure 3.8 shows a different model for the same set of data, utilizing both "Advertising" and "Income" as predictors. Figure 3.9 shows a model for the "House Price" data from Chapter 2. That model uses seven different pieces of information (the square footage, the number of bedrooms and number of bathrooms, the number of offers, whether the siding is brick material, whether the house is located in the North neighborhood, and whether the house is located in the West neighborhood). Since we can include a seemingly endless number of predictors in any regression model, the question arises as to which predictors are important and which predictors add less value to our modeling efforts. We will answer this question next. To that end, we will introduce the concept of "signal-to-noise" ratio, which will allow us to quantify the strength of a predictor's impact relative to its uncertainty.

3.3.1   The Signal-to-Noise Ratio

Figure 3.10 shows three hypothetical data scenarios, labeled as "A", "B," and "C." In each scenario, we see a predictor (X), a response (Y), and the associated data cloud between X and Y. Which of these three scenarios corresponds to the strongest relationship between X and Y?

```
Coefficients:
                   Estimate Std. Error t value Pr(>|t|)
(Intercept)         598.919   9552.197   0.063 0.950110
SqFt                 52.994      5.734   9.242 1.10e-15 ***
Bedrooms           4246.794   1597.911   2.658 0.008939 **
Bathrooms          7883.278   2117.035   3.724 0.000300 ***
Offers            -8267.488   1084.777  -7.621 6.47e-12 ***
BrickYes          17297.350   1981.616   8.729 1.78e-14 ***
NeighborhoodNorth  1560.579   2396.765   0.651 0.516215
NeighborhoodWest  22241.616   2531.758   8.785 1.32e-14 ***
---
Signif. codes:  0 '***' 0.001 '**' 0.01 '*' 0.05 '.' 0.1 ' ' 1

Residual standard error: 10020 on 120 degrees of freedom
Multiple R-squared: 0.8686,    Adjusted R-squared: 0.861
F-statistic: 113.3 on 7 and 120 DF,  p-value: < 2.2e-16
```

Fig. 3.9 A regression model for the house price data.

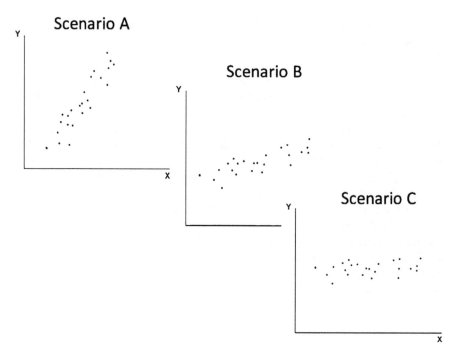

Fig. 3.10 Three hypothetical data examples.

Most of you will probably answer "Scenario A" – but why? Note that the data cloud is the same in all three scenarios except for its rotation relative to X and Y. In other words, while the variation (or the "noise") is identical in all three scenarios, the pattern (or the "signal") varies. Scenario A has the strongest signal (i.e., the steepest trend), while the signal is weakest in Scenario C, which shows barely any trend at all. Scenario B has a discernable trend, but we would not consider the overall relationship as extraordinarily strong because there is significant variation (i.e., noise) around this trend. In other words, the strength of the relationship is captured by the magnitude of the signal *relative* to the noise, or the *signal-to-noise* ratio.

We can measure the signal-to-noise ratio in the following way. The signal is equivalent to the steepness of the observable trend and hence is given by the slope of the associated regression model. Remember that the slope corresponds to the "estimate" (or "coefficient") of the regression model. In Figure 3.9, all slopes are given in the second column (marked as "Estimate"). In order to quantify the noise, regression also provides a solution. The third column in Figure 3.9 provides the "Standard Errors," which essentially measure the variation around the slope, or the noise. We can thus compute the signal-to-noise ratio for the variable square footage (SqFt) as $52.994/5.734 = 9.242$. In other words, the signal of square footage is more than nine times higher than its noise (for this particular set of data). Intuitively, it seems that a signal-to-noise ratio of nine or more must be very good – and our intuition proves right. However, in order to quantify exactly how good a particular signal-to-noise ratio really is, we need the concept of statistical significance and the *p-value*.

3.3.2 Testing for Statistical Significance

Different variables result in different signal-to-noise ratios. For instance, in Figure 3.9, while square footage has a signal-to-noise ratio of more than nine, the variable "bedrooms" has a signal-to-noise ratio of less than three (4246.794/1597.911 = 2.6577). This implies that the relationship between square footage and house prices is stronger than that of bedrooms and house prices. However, does this also imply that, for all practical purposes, bedrooms are unimportant for predicting house prices? In order to make this conclusion, we need a cutoff value, one that determines which signal-to-noise ratios result in important relationships and which ones indicate unimportant relationships. To that end, statistics uses the concept of *p-values*. A *p*-value essentially measures the probability that, given the current information, a particular predictor has no relationship with the response. The *lower the p-value* (i.e., the lower this probability), the *higher the statistical importance* of this predictor. We can also think about a *p*-value from the point of view of a signal-to-noise ratio: the *p*-value measures the probability that, given a particular set of data, the observed signal could have occurred simply due to random chance. The smaller this probability, the more confident we are that the observed signal is "real."

Consider again the regression model in Figure 3.9. The *p*-values are displayed in the last column, marked by $Pr(>|t|)$. We can see that the *p*-value of square footage is extremely small (less than 1.1×10^{-15}); on the other hand, the *p*-value of bedrooms is significantly larger (0.008939). Typically, we consider a variable as *insignificant* (or statistically unimportant) if the associated *p*-value is larger than 0.05. In that sense, both square footage and bedrooms are significant predictors, yet square footage is statistically *more important* than bedrooms. Glancing further down at the regression model, we can further observe that bathrooms and offers are also statistically significant. However, the North neighborhood is insignificant because its *p*-value is very large (0.516215), much larger than our cutoff of 0.05. So we can conclude that while most variables in Figure 3.9 are statistically important, some are more important than others, as signified by their associated *p*-values. Moreover, the only variable that is *statistically insignificant* is the North neighborhood – hence we could remove that variable from our model and potentially obtain a better model.

3.3.3 Gauging Practical Importance

So far, we have learned how to gauge the signal residing in a predictor relative to its noise and ultimately use that information to decide whether or not a predictor is statistically important. However, just because a predictor is statistically important (i.e., its signal is large relative to its noise) does not imply that it is also *practically useful*. In other words, while statistical importance is a necessary condition for practical importance, it is not sufficient. Take the following example as an illustration.

Suppose we are interested in deciding whether or not to add another bathroom to our house. We believe that the addition of a bathroom only makes sense *economically* if it adds at least $6,000 to the house is value. Considering Figure 3.9, should we add that bathroom? We can see that the slope of the variable bathrooms equals 7,883.278; this implies that, for each additional bathroom, on average the price of the house increases by 7,883. It is important to emphasize that this interpretation holds true only on average: sometimes the extra bathroom will add more than 7,883 in value to the house, but at other times the extra value will be less than 7,883. The reason is the uncertainty (or the noise) in the relationship between bathrooms and home prices. So, how can we quantify this uncertainty and come to a statistically sound decision?

We can use the concept of confidence intervals: we compute a 95% *confidence interval* for the slope of bathrooms as[7]

$$\text{slope of bathrooms} \pm (2)(\text{standard error}) \qquad (3.9)$$

or, filling in the values from Figure 3.9,

$$\$7,883.278 \pm (2)(\$2,117.035) \qquad (3.10)$$

which equals

$$(\$3,649.208, \$12,117.35) \qquad (3.11)$$

In other words, the smallest possible added premium due to an additional bathroom is as low as $3,649.208, which is much lower than our desired value of $6,000; hence we should not add the bathroom to our house.

In conclusion, we have seen in this section that in order to make decisions we need to take into account both the signal and the noise of a predictor. The signal is given by the slope; the noise is measured by the standard error around the slope. Only the signal in conjunction with the noise gives a complete picture about the usefulness of a predictor. The signal-to-noise ratio allows us to quantify the statistical usefulness of a predictor; if we conclude that a predictor is insignificant, we often exclude it from our model. However, statistical significance is not necessarily equivalent to practical importance. We can judge practical importance by

---

[7]We are applying the concept of confidence intervals below in a slightly inaccurate way: a 95% is computed by adding and subtracting 1.96 times the standard error from the mean; in the confidence interval calculations below, we are using a factor of 2 instead of 1.96. We believe that for quick-and-dirty manual calculations, this rounding does not make much of a difference. However, in order to obtain a precise answer, one should use computerized calculations rather than manual ones.

adding and subtracting twice the noise from the signal in order to obtain confidence intervals. Confidence intervals allow us to judge practical importance in the presence of statistical uncertainty.

Lessons Learned:

- The signal-to-noise ratio quantifies the importance of the relationship between the response (or output) and a predictor (or input) variable. We can compute the signal-to-noise ratio from the estimated slope and standard error of a regression model. Higher signal-to-noise ratios imply larger statistical significance; in other words, the larger the signal (relative to the noise), the smaller the chance that the observed pattern could have occurred merely by chance. Recall that, when dealing with data, patterns can occur only due to chance; for example, if we happen to select an extreme (but otherwise rather a typical) data point in our sample. The signal-to-noise ratio will tell us whether, based on the entire data cloud, the observed pattern appears very likely to be "true."
- In order to quantify the exact amount of this likelihood, we need to compute the p-value. The p-value tells us whether, given the current data, the observed pattern could have occurred merely by chance; smaller values of the p-value show more support in favor of the observed data pattern.
- The p-value provides a cutoff rule for the signal-to-noise ratio. P-values larger than 0.05 are typically associated with variables that are statistically unimportant. Sometimes, we use even smaller cutoff values (such as 0.01 or 0.001), which forces the signal-to-noise ratio to be even stronger. We often remove statistically unimportant variables from a model. Removing statistically unimportant variables may result in a better data fit (i.e., a higher adjusted R-squared).
- Statistical significance is not the same as practical importance. Confidence intervals on the slope can be helpful to gauge practical importance. Typically, variables that are statistically insignificant are also practically unimportant (but there are exceptions to this rule).
- We can compute 95% confidence intervals on the slope by adding and subtracting roughly twice the standard error. This computation is based on a rule of thumb; we can get more accurate confidence intervals by asking the software to directly compute confidence intervals for us.

3.4 Data Case: Understanding Customers' Spending Patterns Using Basic Regression

We now discuss a complete example to illustrate the main ideas of this chapter. Consider again the direct marketing data from Section 2.2. Recall that the direct marketer has collected, among other things, information about customers' spending

```
Call:
lm(formula = AmountSpent ~ Salary + Catalogs + Children)

Residuals:
     Min        1Q    Median       3Q      Max
-1775.92   -348.73   -38.68   255.49  3211.25

Coefficients:
              Estimate Std. Error t value Pr(>|t|)
(Intercept) -4.428e+02  5.372e+01  -8.242 5.29e-16 ***
Salary       2.041e-02  5.929e-04  34.417  < 2e-16 ***
Catalogs     4.770e+01  2.755e+00  17.310  < 2e-16 ***
Children    -1.987e+02  1.709e+01 -11.628  < 2e-16 ***
---
Signif. codes:  0 '***' 0.001 '**' 0.01 '*' 0.05 '.' 0.1 ' ' 1

Residual standard error: 562.5 on 996 degrees of freedom
Multiple R-squared: 0.6584,        Adjusted R-squared: 0.6574
F-statistic:    640 on 3 and 996 DF,   p-value: < 2.2e-16
```

Fig. 3.11 A regression model for the direct marketing data.

behavior (recorded as the amount of money spent in past transactions), their salary, their number of children, and how many catalogs they have received in the past; see also Table 2.6. The direct marketer is interested in understanding why some customers spend more money than others. Is money the only driver of customer spending? In other words, do customers with a higher salary spend more than customers with a lower salary, and do no other factors play a role? If so, the marketer should probably primarily target customers with the highest incomes. But it is also possible that customer spending is affected by additional factors. For instance, while two customers may have the same income, one may spend less than the other because they have a larger family and hence less cash to spend in this particular store. In other words, the number of children may also play a role, and it may have a negative effect on spending. And, finally, the marketer may also be interested in finding out whether his marketing efforts are "effective." That is, he may ask whether for every dollar he spends on creating, printing, and shipping catalogs the return is sufficiently high. We now answer these questions using regression analysis.

Consider Figure 3.11, which shows a regression model pertaining to the above questions. In particular, it shows the results of estimating a regression model with amount spent as the response (or target or output) variable and salary, number of catalogs, and number of children as independent (or predictor or input) variables. Glancing over the regression output in Figure 3.11, we can make the following observations:

- *Model quality*: The model appears to be of reasonable quality, as the R-squared value (0.6584) is relatively high. In fact, this value suggests that almost 66% of the total uncertainty in customers' spending is explained by the model above. In other words, using only three pieces of information (salary, number of children, and number of catalogs), we can capture all but 34% of customers' spending behavior – this appears to be pretty promising.

• *Interpreting the coefficient of salary*: Salary has a positive coefficient. In fact, the slope of salary equals 0.02041, and it is statistically significant. (Note the small *p*-value.) This implies that for every additional salary dollar a customer earns, he spends $0.02 (i.e., 2 cents) with the direct marketer. This supports the marketer's hunch that salary is an important factor in customer spending. It also supports the notion that customers with higher salaries are more lucrative for the marketer. But does every customer spend at the same rate? No. In fact, 0.02 is the average amount a customer spends cut of each additional salary dollar. Some customers spend at a higher rate, others at a lower rate. A 95% confidence interval for the coefficient of salary is

$$0.02041 - 2 \times 0.0005929, 0.02041 + 2 \times 0.0005929$$

or

$$(0.0192242, 0.0215958)$$

This implies that the lowest rate at which a customer spends his salary dollars is 0.019, or 1.9 cents per every dollar earned; the highest spending rate is 0.022, or 2.2 cents for every dollar earned.

• *Interpreting the coefficient of children*: The coefficient for the number of children equals -198.7. First, we note that this value is negative which implies that there is a negative, relationship between the number of children and the amount of money spent. In other words, the more children a customer has, the fewer he will spend with the direct marketer. More precisely, the value of the coefficient equals 198.7, so for every additional child the customer will spend $198.70 *less* with the direct marketer. Or, put differently one more time, a customer with three children will spend $397.40 *less* than a customer with only one child. One possible conclusion for the direct marketer would therefore be to focus his efforts more on those customers with fewer children.

• *Interpreting the coefficient of catalogs*: Note that the coefficient for the number of catalogs equals 47.70. Our first observation is that this value is positive, which implies that the shipment of catalogs has a positive impact on the bottom line. This is encouraging for the marketer's business. But exactly how effective is the shipment of catalogs? We also note that the *p*-value is very small (smaller than $2 * 10^{-16}$), so catalogs is a statistically significant predictor. But is it also practically effective? Using similar arguments as earlier, we can compute a 95% confidence interval as[8]

$$47.70 - 2 \times 2.755, 47.70 + 2 \times 2.755$$

---

[8] We are again using the factor 2 instead of the more accurate 1.96 in the calculations below.

or

$$(42.19, 53.21)$$

What does this confidence interval imply? It implies that, for each catalog that we ship, the additional amount a customer spends is between $42.19 and $53.21. In other words, as long as we make sure that the costs for creating, printing, and shipping the catalog are less than $42, our business is profitable!

One more word of caution: the result above implies that, for each additional catalog that we ship to a customer, the amount she spends is at least $42.19. One may hastily conclude from this finding that we should just ship hundreds or thousands of catalogs to each customer to increase our earnings – but that conclusion is most likely flawed! It is rather unlikely that the *rate of return* remains the same regardless of the total number of catalogs. In other words, while the finding above may be true for five or ten catalogs, taking it to 100 or 1,000 units may be misleading. This is also referred to as *extrapolation* (i.e., the attempt to make estimates outside the range of the actual data). In reality, the "law of diminishing returns" often kicks in, and it may well be that the additional return on 101 shipped catalogs is not much more than with 100 catalogs. In fact, there is an obvious danger of "overflooding" your customer with the same information over and over again, and 100 shipped catalogs may in fact lead to a lower return compared with 10 or 20 catalogs.

- *Interpreting the intercept*: We note that the estimate of the intercept is negative (-442.8) – what does this mean? Strictly speaking, the intercept denotes the average amount of money spent when all other variables are set equal to zero. In other words, the intercept implies that, for a customer with zero salary, zero number of children, and zero catalogs, that customer will "spend" $-$442.80. However, negative spending does not make much sense. In fact, this is an example of an intercept that does not carry any economic interpretation. As a general rule, intercepts in a regression model do not always lend themselves to practically relevant interpretations, and we should not be too surprised if we encounter an intercept that "does not make sense."

We have now made sense of all the information in Figure 3.11. To that end, we have answered many of the marketer's questions. We have concluded that the model is of reasonable quality and that it provides evidence for the fact that salary is a main driver of customer spending. In fact, we have not only provided evidence for this but have also quantified exactly how much each salary dollar drives customer spending. We have also assessed the effect of a customer's family (in particular, the number of children) and found that it has a negative impact on spending. Moreover, we have also used the regression model to quantify the impact of our core business (shipment of catalogs), which will help us gauge the effectiveness of our business strategies. All in all, the regression model has helped us answer a lot of different business-related questions.

Lessons Learned:

- Interpretation of intercept and slopes: We have carefully interpreted all of the slopes (salary, children, and catalogs) in the model. We have discussed their statistical significance (i.e., their signal-to-noise ratio) as well as their practical usefulness (via the computation of confidence intervals). We have also attempted to interpret the intercept and found out that, at least in this example, it does not lend itself to much practical (or economic) insight. A general takeaway is that intercepts of a regression model may not always make much practical sense. In fact, they may not always be statistically significant (i.e., have a small p-value). However, we typically keep the intercept in the model because it often serves a purely mathematical purpose: it helps us obtain a better (and more realistic) fit of our model to the data. Hence, we hardly ever remove the intercept from the model (even if it is insignificant).

- Interpretation of R-squared: We have seen that the R-squared value is rather high (66%) and hence the model appears to provide a rather excellent fit to the data. However, we have not investigated any alternate models (using the same set of data) and hence we cannot yet conclude that this is the *best* model. We can only claim that one model is best once we have investigated all possible alternatives. In this case, there is good reason to believe that a better model could be found: the direct marketing data in Table 2.6 has a total of ten different variables and we have only used four of them (salary, children, catalogs, and spending) in our current model. What about a customer's age or gender? What about the location where a customer lives? All of these variables could provide extra value to our model and could improve its data fit. Unless we investigate these additional options, we cannot conclude to have found the best model.

- Extrapolation: We have also discussed the concept of extrapolation. Extrapolation is an attempt to apply the model too far outside the range of the data. For instance, if your model is based on salaries that range only between $30K and $50k, then you should not attempt to use it to predict at that a salary level of $100K – we simply do not have any information at that salary value. Extrapolation often leads to predictions that are far from the truth. The reason typically is that our model assumes a linear relationship between the predictor and the response; in our example, it assumes that customers' spending grows at the same constant rate for each additional dollar of salary. This may be true when salary increases from $40K to $50K, but does it also hold true for an increase from $100K to $200K? If we do not have any information about the higher salary range ($100K to $200K), then we simply do not know. In reality, the impact of salary on customer spending could change at higher salary levels – it could, for example, slow down (or it could increase). Extrapolation is one of the main dangers of regression models, and we should be careful not to step into this trap.

Chapter 4
Data Modeling II – Making Models More Flexible

In Chapter 3, we introduced the basic concept of a regression model. In fact, we spent quite a lot of time discussing *linear* regression models. Linearity is a basic feature of regression, but it is also one of its main limitations. The reason is that, in practice, linearity is often only an approximation to reality. Many phenomena and processes that occur in nature or in business are not linear at all. When we approximate these processes using a linear regression model, we often trade convenience for accuracy. Indeed, one reason why linear regression models are so widespread and popular is that they are efficient to implement and easy to interpret. However, as a cautious researcher, you should always ask yourself whether the event that you are modeling is truly linear and how much accuracy you are sacrificing by making this assumption.

In many situations, a linear model is a sufficient (and practically satisfactory) approximation to reality. However, there exist plenty of business situations for which this assumption is questionable. Consider for instance the following example. A regression model may tell you that the more you put into advertising, the higher your sales will be. While you generally have no problem believing that this relationship is true for your market, your business sense also tells you that there must be a point after which "more is not always better." In other words, you have a hunch that while more advertising generally results in higher sales, consumers may reach a "saturation point," and, when they reach that point, additional advertising does not add anything to your bottom line. In fact, some may argue that there may even be a point after which consumers get annoyed or frustrated by overexposure to the same ad and any additional advertising may in fact have a negative effect on sales. In other words, sales may increase for certain (lower) levels of advertising, reach a maximum point, and decrease from there on out for any additional (higher) levels of advertising – just like an inverse U-shape.

Saturation points, diminishing returns, or inverse-U shapes cannot be modeled using linear regression – at least not directly. In order to accommodate such effects in our model, we need to make it more *flexible*. There exist many ways of making regression more flexible – some rely on mathematical and computationally complex methodology, and others involve rather quick and simple "tricks." These tricks

W. Jank, *Business Analytics for Managers*, Use R!, DOI 10.1007/978-1-4614-0406-4_4,

revolve around *data transformations* and data recoding, and we will discuss them below in Sections 4.1 and 4.2. Later, in Section 6.2, we will also touch upon some of the computationally more involved methods and compare them against the simpler tricks from this chapter.

4.1   More Flexible Models (1): Dummy Variables and Interaction Terms

In this section, we discuss two of the most important concepts in statistics that help make models more flexible. These are *dummy variables* and *interaction terms*. "Dummy variable" is another name for a binary variable, and it simply refers to a recoding of the data. However, it is important to note that we do not mean just about any recoding of the data – the specific form of the recoding plays an important role. An "interaction term," on the other hand, is simply the multiplication of two variables. While multiplying two variables does not appear to be rocket science, it results in a much more flexible regression model. Indeed, we have already seen that linear models suffer from the fact that they are – oh well – only linear. In fact, a linear relationship between two variables X and Y implies that, for every increase in X, Y also increases, and it increases *at the same rate*. Having a constant rate of increase is a rather strict (and sometimes overly restrictive) assumption. Interaction terms can alleviate that assumption. In fact, interaction terms allow us to *model* the rate of increase as a function of a third variable, say Z. Here are a few more concrete examples to bring the point across: Do you believe that consumers' spending increases with their salary *regardless of their geographical location*? Or, do you find it more plausible that consumers' spending increases *faster* for those who live closer to a relevant store or mall? Another example: Do you think consumers are equally price sensitive, *regardless of the channel*? Or, would you find it more plausible that price sensitivity is *higher* for online sales channels? If you answered "yes" to any of these questions, then you should read on. We will now show how we can get to the bottom of some of these questions using dummy variables and interaction terms.

Gender Discrimination Data: Consider the data in Table 4.1. It shows a snapshot of data pertaining to a possible gender discrimination case. In fact, it shows information about employees' gender (male vs. female), their experience (measured in years), and their annual salary (in US dollars). We are interested in understanding whether the data suggests that there is systematic compensation discrimination against female employees. In other words, all else equal, do female employees earn systematically less than their male counterparts?

Data Exploration: Figure 4.1 gives the first answer to this question. It shows *side-by-side boxplots* of salary, broken up by gender. We can see that the median salary of female employees (the thick solid line in the middle of the box) is significantly lower than for male employees. We can also see that the highest salary levels for female employees are much lower than those of male employees. So, does

Table 4.1 The gender discrimination data. The first column denotes the gender of each employee; the second column denotes the level of experience (in number of years); and the third column denotes the annual salary (in dollars). See also file *Gender Discrimination.csv.*

Gender	Experience	Salary
Male	7	53400
Female	11	53600
Female	6	54000
Male	10	54000
Female	5	57000
Female	6	57000
Female	4	57200
Female	11	57520
Male	3	58000

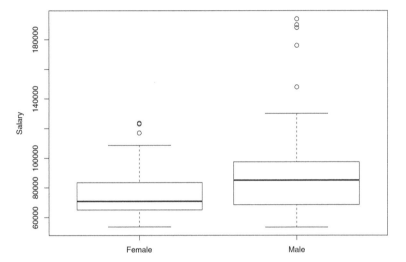

Fig. 4.1 A side-by-side boxplot of salary, broken up by gender.

this finding already suggest systematic discrimination? Maybe, but other factors (factors different from gender) may cause the salary discrepancy. These factors could include, among other things, an employee's level of experience. In fact, could it be that all female employees have lower experience levels and hence explain the lower salaries?

Figure 4.2 gives an answer to that question. It shows side-by-side boxplots of experience, broken up by gender. It appears that experience levels of female employees are not lower than those of male employees. In fact, the median experience level of female employees is *higher* than that of their male counterparts. In other words, low experience levels of female employees cannot be the explanation for their lower salary levels![1]

---

[1] While there could be other explanations for the low salary levels of female employees, such as lower levels of education or lower levels of industry experience, we do not have that information available in our data.

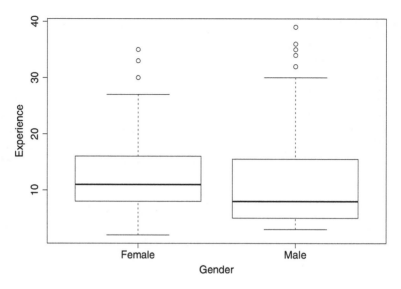

Fig. 4.2   A side-by-side boxplot of experience, broken up by gender.

Simpson's Paradox: One caveat of the boxplots in Figures 4.1 and 4.2 is that they show the information of only two variables at a time (salary and gender in Figure 4.1, experience and gender in Figure 4.2); they cannot simultaneously display the information of a third (and possibly related) variable. In other words, Figure 4.1 shows the relationship between salary and gender but cannot *control* for the impact of experience; similarly, Figure 4.2 shows the relationship between experience and gender without controlling for salary. One problem with such an approach is that the *relationship between two variables can change when introducing a third variable*; this is often referred to as *Simpson's Paradox*.[2] Simpson's Paradox is one reason for the popularity of regression models. In a regression model – unlike in a simple graph – we can *control* for as many variables as we like and thus get a better understanding of the true causal relationship between two variables. Sometimes we can "tweak" existing graphs to make them account for more than two pieces of information at a time. For instance, Figure 4.3 shows a *scatterplot* between two pieces of information, salary and experience. On that plot, we also control for the effect of a third variable (i.e., gender) by marking male employees with triangles and female employees with circles.

Figure 4.3 shows that the *salary pattern* for male employees (triangles) follows a different path than that of female employees (circles). This observation motivates our modeling efforts in the next section. We would like to derive a model that is flexible enough to accommodate and capture these different salary patterns. We will see that we can accomplish this goal with the help of dummy variables and interaction terms.

---

[2]See also http://en.wikipedia.org/wiki/Simpson's_paradox.

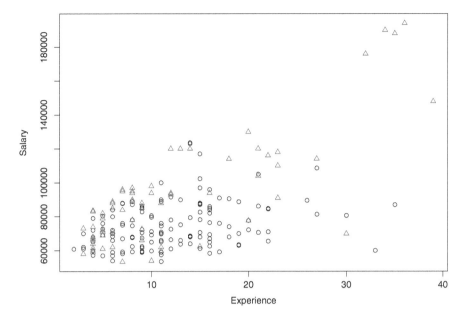

Fig. 4.3 A scatterplot of salary vs. experience; the circles refer to female employees and the triangles are male employees.

4.1.1   Dummy Variables

Consider again the data in Table 4.1. How can we derive a regression model based on this data? While we have already learned how to build a model based on the two (numeric) variables salary and experience, the variable gender is *not* numeric. In fact, gender assumes the values "male" or "female," which are both text strings. How can we incorporate text (i.e., nonnumeric data) into a regression model? The short answer is "We can't" (at least not directly), as regression can only handle numeric data values. This means that we first have to recode the variable gender in such a way that its values become numeric. This can be done in many different ways, but only one way leads to the right answer.

Creating Dummy Variables: Consider the following recoding of the variable gender. Let us define a new variable, *Gender.Male*, as

$$\text{Gender.Male} = \begin{cases} 1, & \text{if gender} = \text{"male"} \\ 0, & \text{otherwise} \end{cases} \tag{4.1}$$

The new variable Gender.Male only assumes values zero and one, so it is numeric. Notice that for a male employee Gender.Male = 1 and for a female employee

```
Call:
lm(formula = Salary ~ Gender.Male)

Residuals:
   Min     1Q Median     3Q    Max
-37611 -12868  -3720   8230 102989

Coefficients:
             Estimate Std. Error t value Pr(>|t|)
(Intercept)     74420       1789  41.597  < 2e-16 ***
Gender.Male     16591       3129   5.302 2.94e-07 ***
---
Signif. codes:  0 `***' 0.001 `**' 0.01 `*' 0.05 `.' 0.1 ` ' 1

Residual standard error: 21170 on 206 degrees of freedom
Multiple R-squared: 0.1201,     Adjusted R-squared: 0.1158
F-statistic: 28.12 on 1 and 206 DF,  p-value: 2.935e-07
```

Fig. 4.4 A regression model with only one dummy variable. The response variable is salary and the predictor Gender.Male is coded as "1" if the gender equals male.

Gender.Male $= 0$, so it carries the same information as the original variable gender. Alternatively, we could have also defined

$$\text{Gender.Female} = \begin{cases} 1, & \text{if gender} = \text{"female"} \\ 0, & \text{otherwise} \end{cases} \quad (4.2)$$

which carries the identical information as Gender.Male. In fact, Gender.Male $= 1 -$ Gender.Female, so we can use either the former or the latter, but we should not use both. Using both Gender.Male and Gender.Female in our regression model simultaneously leads to problems because we are essentially employing the same information twice. This leads to a (mathematical) caveat often referred to as *multicollinearity*.

Dummy Variables and Binary Variables: We also refer to Gender.Male as a *dummy variable* because it does not carry any new information but simply recodes the existing information in a numerical way. Dummy variables are also referred to as binary variables or 0-1 variables.

Interpreting a Dummy Variable Regression Model: Let's look first at a regression model using the dummy variable Gender.Male above. Figure 4.4 shows a regression model with only the gender dummy variable (and salary as the response variable). We can see that Gender.Male is statistically significant. (Notice the small p-value.) We can also see that its estimated coefficient equals 16,591. What does this mean? Strictly speaking, it implies that for every increase in the dummy variable Gender.Male by one unit, salary increases by $16,591. But what does an increase in the gender dummy really mean? The dummy variable only assumes two values, zero and one. So, if we increase its value from zero to one, salary goes up by $16,591. Now if we recall the recoding in equation (4.1), then we can interpret this in the following way:

If we change from a female (Gender.Male = 0) to a male (Gender.Male = 1) employee, then salary increases by $16,591.

In other words, male employees make $16,591 *more* in salary than female employees.

So far, we have only interpreted the meaning of the gender dummy in Figure 4.4. But what about the intercept? The value of the intercept equals 74,420. What does this mean? By definition, it is the value of salary when all other variables in the model are set equal to zero. In that sense, setting *Gender_Male* equal to zero, we can conclude that the salary of female employees is $74,420 on average.

An Incorrect Recoding of the Data: Equation (4.1) codes the information contained in gender in a binary fashion: we assign "1" if the gender is male and "0" if it is female. Another way of thinking about this coding is in the form of a simple "Yes/No" question:

"Is the gender male?"

If the answer is "Yes," then we assign the value "1"; we assign the value "0" if the answer is "No." In other words, we don't really recode the data – all we do is assign a numeric translation of the words "Yes" and "No." That is exactly the idea of binary data.

We pointed out earlier that a different recoding (in fact, any other recoding) can lead to confusion and possibly wrong conclusions. Take the following example as an illustration. Assume that we are coding the gender information in a different way. Define the variable Gender.Male2 as

$$\text{Gender.Male2} = \begin{cases} 400, & \text{if gender} = \text{"male"} \\ -10, & \text{if gender} = \text{"female"} \end{cases} \tag{4.3}$$

Note that there is no reason at all for assigning males the value of 400 and females the value of -10. But inexperienced students often make the mistake of assigning some (i.e. any arbitrary) value to the categorical gender information. What would happen if we used a coding such as in equation (4.3)?

Figure 4.5 shows the regression model based on the recoding in equation (4.3). We can see that the coefficient of gender is now completely different from the one in Figure 4.4. Moreover, how can we interpret the number 553 for Gender.Male2? Salary increases by $553 if we increase what relative to what? This regression model is very hard to interpret and will likely lead to wrong conclusions about the difference between male and female salaries.

Insight about Dummy Variables: We can take away the following insight about dummy variables:

- Dummy variables always conduct *pairwise* comparisons. In the example above, the gender dummy compares the salary of male employees against that of

```
Call:
lm(formula = Salary ~ Gender.Male2)

Residuals:
   Min     1Q Median     3Q    Max
-37611 -12868  -3720   8230 102989

Coefficients:
              Estimate Std. Error t value Pr(>|t|)
(Intercept)    96541.2    3474.3  27.787  < 2e-16 ***
Gender.Male2     553.0     104.3   5.302 2.94e-07 ***
---
Signif. codes:  0 '***' 0.001 '**' 0.01 '*' 0.05 '.' 0.1 ' ' 1

Residual standard error: 21170 on 206 degrees of freedom
Multiple R-squared: 0.1201,     Adjusted R-squared: 0.1158
F-statistic: 28.12 on 1 and 206 DF,  p-value: 2.935e-07
```

Fig. 4.5 A regression model with a different (incorrect) way of recoding the data.

female employees. It does not capture the absolute salary of male employees; rather, it captures the salary premium of male (relative to female) employees. It is important to remember that dummy variables always perform pairwise comparisons.

- When we include a dummy variable in a regression model, the intercept contains the effect of the "baseline." In our example, we defined Gender.Male=1 for male employees; the level that is defined as zero (female in this case) is often referred to as the baseline. The effect of the baseline is contained in the intercept. In our example, the intercept denotes the salary level of female employees.

A More Complex Dummy Variable Regression Model: Figure 4.6 shows a modified regression model. In that model, we have included not only the gender dummy but also the years of experience. We again note that all variables are highly significant (i.e., have small p-values). Moreover, both the gender dummy and experience have positive coefficients (i.e., they have a positive correlation with salary). We now take a closer look at the precise interpretation of the dummy variable Gender.Male. To that end, it is helpful to write out the estimated regression model based on Figure 4.6.

Using Figure 4.6, the regression model equals

$$\text{Salary} = 53{,}260 + 1{,}744.6 \times \text{Experience} + 17{,}020.6 \times \text{Gender.Male} \quad (4.4)$$

How does equation (4.4) help us characterize female employees? Recall that for female employees Gender.Male $= 0$. Setting the dummy equal to zero, the last term in equation (4.4) drops out and we get the *female-specific* regression equation

$$\text{Salary} = 53{,}260 + 1{,}744.6 \times \text{Experience} \quad (4.5)$$

```
Call:
lm(formula = Salary ~ Experience + Gender.Male)

Residuals:
    Min      1Q   Median      3Q      Max
-52779.5  -9806.3   -121.1   8346.8   60912.8

Coefficients:
             Estimate Std. Error t value Pr(>|t|)
(Intercept)   53260.0     2416.6  22.039  < 2e-16 ***
Experience     1744.6      160.7  10.858  < 2e-16 ***
Gender.Male   17020.6     2499.6   6.809 1.06e-10 ***
---
Signif. codes:  0 `***' 0.001 `**' 0.01 `*' 0.05 `.' 0.1 ` ' 1

Residual standard error: 16910 on 205 degrees of freedom
Multiple R-squared: 0.4413,     Adjusted R-squared: 0.4359
F-statistic: 80.98 on 2 and 205 DF,  p-value: < 2.2e-16
```

Fig. 4.6 A second regression model with the gender dummy and level of experience. The response is again salary.

In other words, for females, the intercept equals 53,260 and the experience slope equals 1,744.6. This has the following implications:

- We know that the intercept denotes the salary level for zero years of experience. In other words, female employees with zero years of experience make, on average, $53,260. Or, put differently one more time, the *starting salary* for female employees equals $53,260.
- The coefficient of experience equals 1,744.6. This implies that, for each additional year of experience, salary increases by $1,744.6 for female employees.

How do the results differ for male employees? For male employees, if we set Gender.Male $= 1$ in equation (4.4), we get the *male-specific* regression equation

$$\text{Salary} = (53,260 + 17,020.6) + 1,744.6 \times \text{Experience} \qquad (4.6)$$

or

$$\text{Salary} = 70,280.6 + 1,744.6 \times \text{Experience} \qquad (4.7)$$

We can summarize the implications of equation (4.7) as follows:

- The intercept (70,280.6) implies that the *starting salary* for male employees equals $70,280.6, or $17,020.6 more than female employees.
- The coefficient of experience equals 1,744.6, which is the same as for female employees. This implies that, for each additional year of experience, the salary of male employees increases by $1,744.6. It is important to note that this salary increase is the same for male and female employees.

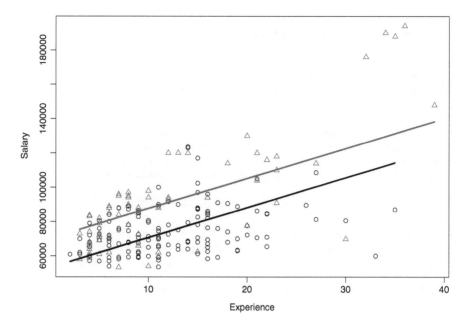

Fig. 4.7 A scatterplot of salary vs. experience; the circles again refer to female employees and the triangles are for male employees. The two solid lines show the estimated dummy variable regression model. Since the lines are parallel, we can conclude that the slopes are identical, only the intercepts differ.

So what do the results in equations (4.5) and (4.7) imply? First, they imply that although we are fitting a single regression model, we are de facto allowing for two separate salary vs. experience relationships, one for female employees and another one for male employees. But exactly how different are those two relationships? We have pointed out above that the impact of experience is the same for both male and female employees. In other words, the incremental impact of an additional year of experience is, at least as per our model, identical for male and female employees. The only difference lies in the intercept (i.e., in the starting salary). In fact, we have seen that, as per our model, the starting salary is higher for male employees than for their female counterparts.

Takeaways: To summarize, our dummy variable regression model allows us to capture different data patterns for male and female employees. However, the only difference is in terms of the intercept; the slope of both data patterns is the same. This point is emphasized in Figure 4.7, which shows the *estimated regression lines* for male and female employees. We can see that the lines are parallel (i.e., they differ only in the intercept, not in the slope). So the takeaway is that, by including a dummy variable in a regression model, we can increase its flexibility by allowing for data trends with different intercepts (but the same slopes).

4.1.2   Interaction Terms

Figure 4.7 shows that dummy variable regression models result in increased flexibility and better capture the varying data patterns for male and female employees. However, a closer inspection of Figure 4.7 also raises the question of whether parallel lines are really the best representation of the observed data. In other words, doesn't it appear as if for every additional year of experience salary for male employees grows at a *faster rate* than that of female employees? If that was the case, wouldn't that necessitate a model that allows for lines that are *not parallel*? Non-parallel lines imply slopes that vary – but how can we introduce varying slopes into our regression model? The answer can be found in the concept of *interaction terms*.

Creating Interaction Terms: An interaction term is simply the multiplication of two variables. In our example, if we multiply the dummy variable Gender.Male with Experience, we get

$$\text{Gender.Exp.Int} = \text{Gender.Male} \times \text{Experience} \tag{4.8}$$

and we refer to this new variable as "Gender.Exp.Int," but we could have chosen any other name. For illustration, consider the first three rows of data from Table 4.1. The dummy variable assumes the values

$$\text{Gender.Male} = \begin{pmatrix} 1 \\ 0 \\ 0 \end{pmatrix} \tag{4.9}$$

while experience assumes the values

$$\text{Experience} = \begin{pmatrix} 7 \\ 11 \\ 6 \end{pmatrix} \tag{4.10}$$

Thus, the (row-by-row) multiplication of Gender.Male and Experience gives

$$\text{Gender.Male} \times \text{Experience} = \begin{pmatrix} 1 \times 7 \\ 0 \times 11 \\ 0 \times 6 \end{pmatrix} \tag{4.11}$$

or

$$\text{Gender.Exp.Int} = \begin{pmatrix} 7 \\ 0 \\ 0 \end{pmatrix} \tag{4.12}$$

```
Call:
lm(formula = Salary ~ Experience + Gender.Male + Gender.Exp.Int

Residuals:
    Min      1Q Median      3Q     Max
 -71048   -9278   -1701   9166   47932

Coefficients:
                 Estimate Std. Error t value Pr(>|t|)
(Intercept)       66333.6     2811.7  23.592  < 2e-16 ***
Experience          666.7      206.5   3.228  0.00145 **
Gender.Male       -8034.3     4110.6  -1.955  0.05201 .
Gender.Exp.Int     2086.2      287.3   7.261 7.95e-12 ***
---
Signif. codes:  0 '***' 0.001 '**' 0.01 '*' 0.05 '.' 0.1 ' ' 1

Residual standard error: 15110 on 204 degrees of freedom
Multiple R-squared: 0.5561,      Adjusted R-squared: 0.5495
F-statistic: 85.18 on 3 and 204 DF,   p-value: < 2.2e-16
```

Fig. 4.8 A regression model using an interaction term. The model includes the gender dummy, the level of experience, and the interaction between the two. The response is again salary.

That's it. There's no rocket science behind the creation of interaction terms. However, while it is straightforward to create interaction terms, their interpretation is a little more involved. We will get to this next.

Interpreting Interaction Terms: Figure 4.8 shows a regression model using the interaction term above. The model also includes both the gender dummy variable and the years of experience. The response is again salary.

We can make several high-level observations. Compared with the previous models in Figure 4.4 and Figure 4.6, this model provides a better fit to the data, as the value of R-squared is now significantly higher. In fact, while R-squared equals only 12.01% in Figure 4.4 (first model), it increases to 44.13% in Figure 4.6 (second model). However, the model with the interaction term (current model) provides an even better fit, as the R-squared value in Figure 4.8 equals 55.61%. We can also see that not all the variables in Figure 4.8 are equally significant. In fact, while the p-value of the interaction term is very low (i.e., Gender.Exp.Int is highly significant), the p-value of the dummy variable is rather large and hence Gender.Male is only borderline significant. It is also interesting to note that the *sign* of the dummy variable has changed: while it was positive in Figure 4.4 and Figure 4.6, it is negative for the model including the interaction term.

But what exactly is the insight generated by the regression model in Figure 4.8? To answer that question, it is again helpful to write out the associated regression equation. Using the same idea as in equation (4.4), we can write

$$\text{Salary} = 66{,}333.6 + 666.7 \times \text{Experience} - 8{,}034.3 \times \text{Gender.Male}$$

$$+ 2{,}086.2 \times \text{Gender.Exp.Int} \tag{4.13}$$

From this equation, we will again derive the equation pertaining specifically to male and female employees, respectively.

For females, we again set the dummy variable equal to zero. Setting Gender.Male $= 0$, the last two terms in equation (4.13) drop out and we obtain

$$\text{Salary} = 66{,}333.6 + 666.7 \times \text{Experience} \qquad (4.14)$$

In other words, for females, the intercept now equals 66,333.6 and the experience slope equals 666.7. This has the following implications:

- As the intercept denotes the salary for employees with zero years of experience in the female-specific model above, we can conclude that the *starting salary* for female employees equals \$66,333.6.
- The coefficient for experience equals 666.7 in the female-specific model above. This implies that, for female employees, salary increases by \$666.7 for each additional year of experience.

How is this different for male employees? Using the same rationale, we now set Gender.Male $= 1$ in equation (4.13) to obtain

$$\text{Salary} = 66{,}333.6 + 666.7 \times \text{Experience} - 8{,}034.3 \times 1 + 2{,}086.2 \times 1 \times \text{Experience}$$

$$(4.15)$$

Notice that the last term equals $2{,}086.2 \times 1 \times \text{Experience}$ since we plug "1" into the interaction term between Gender.Male and Experience; moreover, since the interaction is the multiplication between these two terms, this yields $1 \times \text{Experience}$. Equation (4.15) now has many related terms, and we can clean them up as

$$\text{Salary} = (66{,}333.6 - 8{,}034.3) + (666.7 + 2{,}086.2) \times \text{Experience} \qquad (4.16)$$

or

$$\text{Salary} = 58{,}299.3 + 2{,}752.9 \times \text{Experience} \qquad (4.17)$$

Based on this equation, we can derive the following insight for male employees:

- The intercept equals 58,299.3 in the male-specific model above, which is lower than that of female employees. In other words, the *starting salary* for males equals \$58,299.3, which is a lower starting salary than for female employees.
- The slope for experience equals 2,752.6 in the male-specific model above. This slope is much larger than for female employees. In other words, the *rate of salary increase* for male employees equals \$2,752.6 for each additional year of experience. This implies that male employees earn *much faster* (as a function of their experience) than female employees.

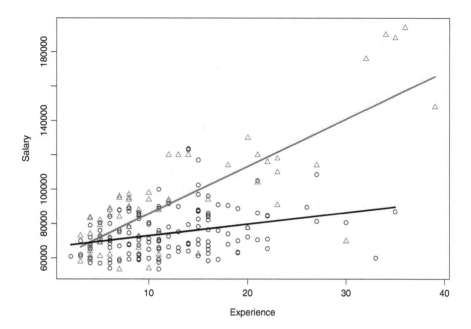

Fig. 4.9 A scatterplot of salary vs. experience; the circles again refer to female employees and the triangles are for male employees. The two solid lines show the estimated dummy variable regression model. Now the lines are no longer parallel, which implies that both the slopes and intercepts differ.

- Summarizing both points, we can conclude that while there does not appear to exist any discrimination in terms of starting salary, male employees earn salary faster for each additional year of experience.

Takeaways: We can summarize our insight from the regression model with interaction terms as follows. The interaction term allows for both varying intercepts and varying slopes. This implies that although we are only fitting one regression model, the resulting model is variable enough to accommodate quite heterogeneous data patterns. These varying data patterns could be interpreted as heterogeneous subsegments in the data. For instance, the relationship between experience and salary could be different for male and female employees. Indeed, Figure 4.9 shows the estimated regression model. We can see that the data pattern for female employees is very different from that of male employees: while female salaries (black circles) grow very slow for every year of experience, male salaries (red triangles) increase at a much steeper rate. The model based on interaction terms captures this heterogeneity in the data slopes and, as pointed out earlier, results in a model that provides a much better fit (in terms of R-squared) to the data.

> **Lessons Learned:**
>
> - Before incorporating categorical data (e.g., responses recorded as text) into a regression model, we have to recode the data to a numerical format. Recoding should only be done in a binary fashion (i.e., via the creation of dummy variables). If we have a data vector with m different categories, then we need $(m-1)$ dummy variables to capture its information. Using a coding different from the dummy variable can lead to potentially wrong conclusions and decisions.
> - Incorporating dummy variables into a regression model renders more flexible modeling options. Using a dummy variable together with another numerical predictor, we can model data trends that resemble parallel lines (i.e., lines with the same slope but a different intercept).
> - Interaction terms can further increase the flexibility of regression. An interaction term is simply the multiplication of two numerical variables. Interaction terms allow for varying slopes in the data.
> - Interpreting interaction terms has to be done with care. Models with a dummy variable, a numerical variable, and the interaction between both variables allow us to model data trends that resemble nonparallel lines. In other words, such models allow us to capture trends with different slopes and intercepts.

4.2   More Flexible Models (2): Nonlinear Relationships and Data Transformations

We have seen in Section 4.1 that by using dummy variables and interaction terms we can make regression models more flexible by incorporating data patterns with varying intercepts and slopes. However, while this greatly improves the flexibility of the *basic* regression model from Chapter 3, one limitation is that the data patterns we can capture are still only *linear* in nature. In other words, using dummy variables and interaction terms, we cannot capture trends that do not behave in a linear   fashion. Take a look at Figure 4.10, which provides another perspective on the discrimination data from Table 4.1. In that figure, we have overlaid the observed data with two smooth trend lines.[3] The most important feature of these two smooth trend lines is that they are no longer required to be straight (or linear); i.e., they are flexible and are allowed to   capture *slope changes* in the data. In fact, the smooth trend lines suggest that the rate of salary increase is quite different for male and female employees: while the salary of female employees (bottom line; black) grows at a barely noticeable pace, that of male employees (top line; red) grows much faster.

---

[3]Both trend lines were created with the help of so-called *smoothing splines*; see, e.g., http://en.wikipedia.org/wiki/Smoothing_spline.

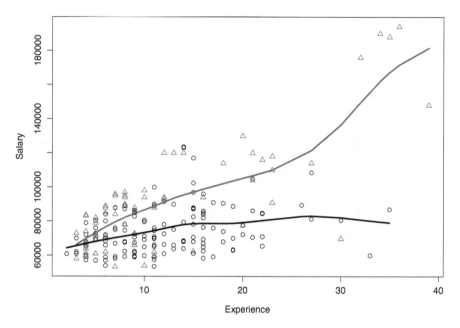

Fig. 4.10 Another take on the discrimination data from Table 4.1. Both trend lines are created using so-called smoothing splines. They suggest that salary does not increase linearly and that the rate of salary increase changes from year to year.

In fact, while male salary initially grows at a somewhat moderate pace (until about 28 years of experience), it takes off rather rapidly for experience levels between 30 and 40 years. In other words, the rate of salary increase *does not remain constant* for male employees, and it is much faster in later years.

What does the observation above suggest? It suggests that the pattern residing in the discrimination data may not be linear after all. So, should we apply a linear model to data that is obviously nonlinear? What would be the consequences of *oversimplifying* our data and approximating nonlinear data patterns with a linear model? There is no general answer to these questions, and our conclusions may change on a case-by-case basis. In some cases, a linear model may serve our purpose just fine and may lead to satisfactory (and practically useful) results; in other cases, however, ignoring nonlinearity in the data may lead to wrong conclusions, predictions, and forecasts, and ultimately to wrong managerial decisions.

Price and Demand Data: Consider the data in Table 4.2. It shows weekly prices for a certain household detergent together with the associated weekly demand (or quantity sold), measured in thousands of units. We can see that prices fluctuate from week to week. In some weeks, the price is as low as $4.10; in other weeks, the price is as high as $5.42. As expected from basic price and demand economics, we observe that demand is higher in weeks where prices are low and it is lower when the price increases. In other words, if we plotted the data in Table 4.2 on a

Table 4.2 Price and demand data. The first column shows the price for a certain household detergent (in US dollars); the second column shows the associated quantity sold (in thousands). See also file *PriceAndDemand.csv*.

Price	Qty
4.51	1637
4.25	1731
4.34	1625
4.31	2119
4.1	1841
4.81	1843
5.19	1121
5.42	1487
4.69	1841
5.98	1071

scatterplot, then we would expect to see a *negative* relationship between price and demand. However, would we expect that relationship to be *linear*? That is, would you expect that a change in price always carries the same effect on the change in demand, *regardless of the current price-level*?

Consider the following scenario: Suppose the current price is $4.50 and you consider increasing the price by $0.10 in the following week. What would you expect? You would probably expect the demand to decrease slightly for that week. Now, what if the current price was set at $10 and you again debate whether or not to increase it by $0.10. Would you expect to see the same demand decrease as in the previous scenario? Probably not. But why? One reason is that at a price of $10, hardly anyone is buying your product anyway[4] (i.e., your demand is already (almost) zero). So, increasing the price by $0.10 (i.e., from $10 to $10.10) will not have much of an impact, as your demand cannot decrease much further (since it is already almost equal to zero)!

Nonlinear Regression Models: The example above suggests that in some scenarios it would be desirable to have a model that allows the effect of a change in X (e.g., price) to depend on the *level* of X. Linear models cannot accomplish that because by the very nature of linearity a small increase in X will always have the same effect on Y (e.g., demand), *regardless of the level of X*. So, what we need is a *nonlinear* model. There exist a plethora of   nonlinear models in statistics. Examples include the *logistic regression* model and the *Poisson regression* model. In this section, we will only focus on approaches that "trick" the basic (i.e., linear) regression model into becoming nonlinear via a simple   data transformation. We refer to this as a "trick" because the resulting model is, at least strictly speaking, not really nonlinear; in fact, it is a linear model applied to a transformed set of data. However, for the purpose of allowing for more flexible modeling alternatives, this trick is extremely powerful.

The most important consideration *before* resorting to nonlinear modeling alternatives is to decide whether or not such a model is really necessary. To that end,

---

[4]Reasons may include the market value of your product and competitors who charge a much lower price.

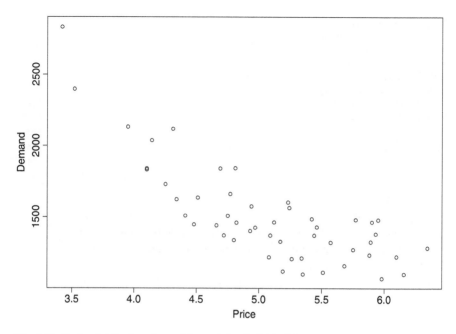

Fig. 4.11 Scatterplot for the price and demand data in Table 4.2.

a graph (together with domain knowledge and practical experience) is invaluable and indispensable. Consider Figure 4.11. It shows a scatterplot for the price and demand data in Table 4.2. We can see that while there is a negative relationship between price and demand (i.e., demand decreases with increasing price), the *slope* of that relationship does not remain constant for all price levels. In fact, it appears as if for lower levels of price (between \$3.50 and \$4.50) demand decays more rapidly; however, demand remains rather stagnant (and low) for higher levels of price (at \$5.00 and above). This suggests that a linear model would not be the best representation of this data. In fact, it suggests that we should look for a nonlinear regression model!

To drive this point home one more time, Figure 4.12 shows the same data as in Figure 4.11, but now we also overlay a linear regression model based on the data (black solid line) as well as a smooth trendline (grey dashed line). The smooth trendline captures the overall pattern in the data much better than the linear model, and it suggests that the data pattern is not linear at all. In fact, if we were to apply the linear regression model to this data, then we would severely *underestimate* the true price-and-demand relationship at the margins of the data cloud (i.e., below \$4.00 and above \$6.00) but *overestimate* it in the center of the data (between \$4.50 and \$5.50). In other words, if our pricing decisions were to rely on a linear regression model, then we would *always* make the wrong decision: sometimes our model would be overly optimistic and other times it would be too pessimistic – and we would never know the direction and the magnitude of the error and would ultimately doom the performance of our product.

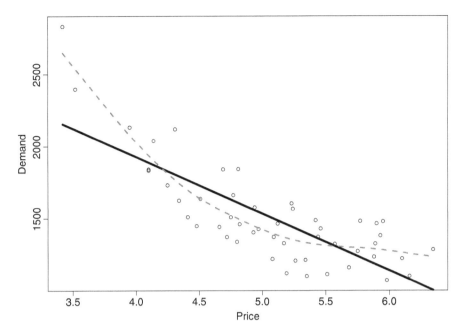

Fig. 4.12 Scatterplot for the price and demand data in Table 4.2 together with a linear regression model (black solid line) and a smooth trend line (grey dashed line).

4.2.1   *Data Transformations*

How can we find a model that can capture the (nonlinear) data pattern in Figure 4.12? One of the simplest – and often most effective – ways is via a transformation of the data. By "transformation" we mean that we apply a mathematical function to the original data values and then operate on these new data values.

Transformation Example: Consider the following simple example of a data transformation. Suppose we have three data values

$$\begin{pmatrix} 2 \\ 5 \\ 7.1 \end{pmatrix} \tag{4.18}$$

One possible transformation would be to *square* all values. In other words, the data transformation "square" would result in the (new) values

$$\begin{pmatrix} 2^2 \\ 5^2 \\ (7.1)^2 \end{pmatrix} = \begin{pmatrix} 4 \\ 25 \\ 50.41 \end{pmatrix} \tag{4.19}$$

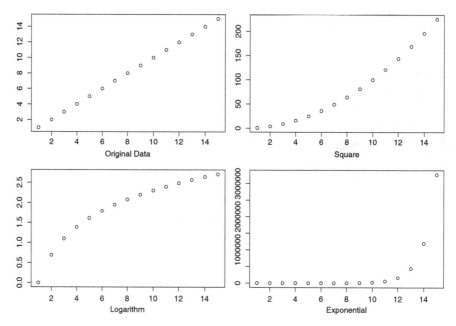

Fig. 4.13 Examples of data transformations: square (top right), logarithmic (bottom left), and exponential (bottom right).

Another possible (and very common) transformation is the *natural logarithm,* or "log." Applying the log-transformation to the data in (4.18) yields

$$\begin{pmatrix} \log(2) \\ \log(5) \\ \log(7.1) \end{pmatrix} = \begin{pmatrix} 0.6931 \\ 1.3863 \\ 1.9601 \end{pmatrix} \tag{4.20}$$

Common Transformations: We can apply just about any mathematical function from elementary calculus to our data. For instance, we could apply an *inverse transformation*, a *sinusoidal transformation*, or a *Gamma function* to our data. The most common transformations are:

- Polynomials such as X^2, X^3, X^4, etc.
- The logarithmic function $\log(X)$, and its inverse, the exponential function $\exp(X)$.

Figure 4.13 illustrates the shapes of different data transformations.

Transforming the Price and Demand Data: We argued earlier that a linear model does not capture the pattern of the price and demand data in Table 4.2 well. So, what transformation should we apply? In order to arrive at an answer, trial and error is often necessary, at least for the inexperienced user. Experienced users

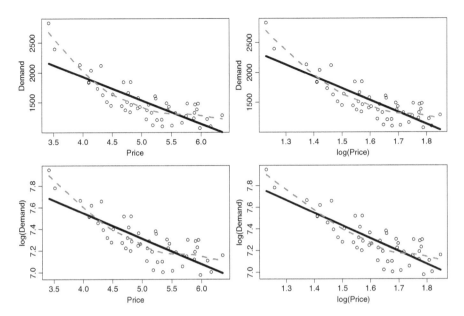

Fig. 4.14 The price and demand data from Table 4.2 in its original form (top left panel) as well as different data transformations. Top right: Demand vs. log(Price); bottom left: log(Demand) vs. Price; bottom right: log(Demand) vs. log(Price).

of data transformation and experts in data modeling often "see" the appropriate transformation when inspecting a scatterplot such as in Figure 4.11. If you don't see that transformation right away, trying out several different options is a smart strategy. Figure 4.14 shows three different transformations for the price and demand data. It shows the original data in the top left panel; the top right panel shows a scatterplot for demand vs. log-transformed price (i.e., log(Price)); the bottom left corner shows the effect of a log-transformation applied to demand, leaving price at its original value; and the bottom right panel shows the effect of applying a log-transformation to both demand and price.

There are several takeaways from Figure 4.14:

- The first is that we can transform more than one variable at a time. While the top right and bottom left panels show the result of applying the log-transformation to only one variable at a time, we transform *both* variables in the bottom right corner of Figure 4.14. When applying data transformations, we can transform as many (or as few) variables as we like.
- Figure 4.14 shows that the shape of the data pattern changes as we apply different transformations. The goal is to find a transformation (or a set of transformations) that render the overall pattern as close to linear (i.e., a straight line) as possible. We can see that none of the three transformations is perfect. However, it appears as if the log-log transformation (i.e., log(Price) and log(Demand)) in the bottom right corner gets closest to a straight line.

```
Call:
lm(formula = log(Qty) ~ log(Price))

Residuals:
     Min       1Q    Median        3Q       Max
-0.23437 -0.08880 -0.00340   0.09432   0.20485

Coefficients:
             Estimate Std. Error t value Pr(>|t|)
(Intercept)    9.2011     0.1946  47.273  < 2e-16 ***
log(Price)    -1.1810     0.1202  -9.822 4.55e-13 ***
---
Signif. codes:  0 '***' 0.001 '**' 0.01 '*' 0.05 '.' 0.1 ' ' 1

Residual standard error: 0.12 on 48 degrees of freedom
Multiple R-squared: 0.6677,     Adjusted R-squared: 0.6608
F-statistic: 96.46 on 1 and 48 DF,  p-value: 4.552e-13
```

Fig. 4.15 A nonlinear regression model. Both price and demand are log-transformed.

Once we identify the best transformation of our data, we input the *transformed* variables into our regression model. That is, instead of modeling

$$\text{Demand} = a + b \times \text{Price} \tag{4.21}$$

we now model

$$\log(\text{Demand}) = a + b \times \log(\text{Price}) \tag{4.22}$$

Or, put differently one more time, rather than applying a linear model to price and demand, we apply it to their transformed values, log(Price) and log(Demand). So in essence we are not really applying a new statistical technique – we are still using the same linear regression model from Chapter 3. Rather, we create new (or transformed) data values and then apply them to linear regression. While the statistical mechanics of this step are rather straightforward and mundane, the challenge lies in *interpreting* the results of a regression model with transformed variables. We will discuss this next.

4.2.2   Interpreting Nonlinear Regression Models

The log-log Regression Model: Figure 4.15 shows the estimated regression model for the log-log transformation in the bottom right corner of Figure 4.14. That is, we first transformed both price and demand using the log-transformation and then fitted a linear regression model to the transformed data values. What does this model imply? A quick inspection of the regression output reveals the following (usual) conclusions:

- *Model fit*: R-squared equals 66.77%, which appears reasonably high. We can thus conclude that a model with (log-) price as the predictor explains almost 67% of all the (log-) demand variation. Notice that R-squared may change if we use price instead of its log-transformed values.
- *Statistical importance*: The p-value of log(Price) is very small. (In fact, it equals 4.55×10^{-13}.) This implies that (log) price is statistically very significant. In other words, the signal is very strong relative to the noise, suggesting that there is a lot of statistical evidence that the relationship is "true" (rather than an artifact of noise).
- *Direction of the relationship*: The sign of the coefficient of log(Price) is negative. This implies that there is a negative relationship between (log-) price and (log-) demand. This relationship is expected from economic considerations and also from our earlier graphical explorations in Figure 4.11.

Is there anything else we can deduce from Figure 4.15? Yes, indeed. So far, we have only concluded about the *sign* of the relationship between price and demand; we have not yet investigated its *magnitude*. In order to investigate the magnitude of that relationship, we consider the value of the coefficient of (log-) price: -1.1810. What does this value mean? If we strictly apply the basic principles of linear regression, then it implies:

For every increase in price by one log-dollar, demand decreases by 1.1810 log-units!

Notice that, in the regression in Figure 4.15, both price and demand are measured in log-units; hence we have to interpret the resulting coefficients on the same scale. But does it make any sense to talk about a log-dollar? Or a log-unit? Hardly! In fact, you will have a very hard time explaining the managerial impact of a log-dollar to your boss or your client! Does this imply that the regression model in Figure 4.15 is not very useful in practice? Or can we interpret its result in another (managerially more intuitive) manner?

In order to derive a more intuitive interpretation of the log-log regression model, we have to take a quick detour into calculus. Notice that we would like to quantify the *change in demand* based on a *small change in price*. In calculus, a small change is typically denoted by the symbol d. So, the change of demand *relative* to the change of price can be written as

$$\frac{d\text{Demand}}{d\text{Price}} \tag{4.23}$$

The equation in (4.23) is often interpreted as the *derivative*. For instance, for a function $f(x)$,

$$\frac{df}{dx} \tag{4.24}$$

denotes the derivative of f with respect to x. Notice that f is a function of x. So, what is the function f in our case? Remember that, as per our regression model,

$$\log(\text{Demand}) = a + b \times \log(\text{Price}) \tag{4.25}$$

or, applying the inverse of the logarithm (i.e., the exponential function), we get

$$\text{Demand} = e^{a+b\times\log(\text{Price})} \tag{4.26}$$

In other words, demand is a function of price, and its precise form is given in equation (4.26).

Let us now consider the derivative of the demand function in (4.26). After a bit of calculus, we obtain

$$\frac{d\text{Demand}}{d\text{Price}} = b \times \frac{\text{Demand}}{\text{Price}} \tag{4.27}$$

We can rearrange equation (4.27) a little more to obtain

$$\frac{d\text{Demand}}{\text{Demand}} = b \times \frac{d\text{Price}}{\text{Price}} \tag{4.28}$$

What does this equation tell us? Notice that

$$\frac{d\text{Demand}}{\text{Demand}} \tag{4.29}$$

can be interpreted as a "small change in demand relative to the current demand value." Similarly,

$$\frac{d\text{Price}}{\text{Price}} \tag{4.30}$$

denotes a "small change in price relative to the current price level." Moreover, b in equation (4.28) denotes the coefficient of log(price) in Figure 4.15, and it links the *relative change in demand* to the *relative change in price*.

We can now put all of the pieces together in the following way. Notice that b equals -1.1810 in Figure 4.15. This implies that:

If we increase price by 1%, then demand decreases by 1.1810%.

In other words, a small proportional change in price results in a small proportional change in demand, and the coefficient of log-price tells us the relationship between these proportional changes. We also note that b is often referred to as the *price elasticity of demand*. In other words, a simple transformation to both price and demand has rendered our simple linear regression model one of the most important models in economics: the price elasticity of demand.[5]

Lessons Learned:

- Not all practically relevant relationships can be modeled in a linear fashion. In fact, most relationships that occur in business and economics are *not* linear at all; however, unless the pattern deviates clearly from linearity, a linear regression model often provides a satisfactory approximation to the underlying truth.

---

[5] See also http://en.wikipedia.org/wiki/Price_elasticity_of_demand.

- Some relationships in business and economics are clearly nonlinear. We can identify these relationships via a combination of domain knowledge, practical experience, and data exploration. The most common exploratory tool to identify nonlinear data patterns is the scatterplot. In fact, since we often do not have a clear hunch about the true relationships in the data, exploratory tools (such as the scatterplot or other graphical solutions introduced in Chapter 2) are indispensable for arriving at realistic and practically useful models.
- Once we identify a nonlinear relationship in the data, we must model it using nonlinear regression methods. There exist many approaches for fitting non-linear regression models. The most straightforward approach is to identify a suitable data transformation.
- There exist many different ways of transforming data, including polynomials such as X^2 or X^3, or logarithmic or exponential transformations. The goal is to transform one (or more) variables such that the resulting data patterns look linear. Data transformation can involve a bit of trial and error. In the process, one should continuously inspect scatterplots and similar tools in order to identify the most suitable transformation. We can also compare the model fit statistics (such as R-squared values) to identify the data transformation that provides a model with the best fit to the data.
- Once we identify the appropriate data transformation, we apply linear regression methods to the transformed data values. While the basic principles of linear regression remain intact (such as interpretations of R-squared or p-values), special attention has to be paid to the interpretation of the resulting coefficients. For instance, in the case of a log-log transformation, the regression coefficient is interpreted in terms of the *elasticities* between input and output variables.

4.3   Data Case: Using Interaction Terms and Data Transformations to Better Understand Customers' Spending Patterns

We now take another look at the direct marketing data from Section 2.6. Recall that we already took a first stab at modeling that data in Section 3.4. However, in that first attempt, we only had available basic regression concepts. We now want to illustrate how we can improve the insight gleaned from that data using the concepts of dummy variables, interaction terms, and data transformations discussed in Sections 4.1 and 4.2. Another takeaway from what follows is that we do not have to treat interaction terms and data transformations as conceptual silos. Many applications call for the *simultaneous* use of different statistical ideas. For instance, it often makes sense to use both interaction terms and data transformation within the *same* statistical model. This will be illustrated next.

Managerial Questions: Recall that the direct marketing data in Table 2.6 contains ten different pieces of information: a customer's demographics (age, gender, marital status, and number of children), whether the customer owns or rents a home, whether the home is close to or far from a store selling similar items, and the customer's salary, purchase history, number of catalogs received, and the amount of money spent at the store. In the following, we are interested in carefully scrutinizing only three out of these ten pieces of information: the customer's salary, location, and the impact of both on the amount of money spent at the store. In particular, we are interested in finding answers to the following questions:

- How does salary relate to a customer's spending? Is the relationship linear? Or does a nonlinear model better capture the impact of salary on a customer's spending pattern?
- How does a customer's location relative to a store (i.e., close vs. far) impact his spending? Do customers who live *farther* from a brick-and-mortar store that sells similar items spend *more*?
- Does the rate of a customer's spending depend on his location? In other words, do customers who live farther away spend their money at a *faster* rate?

Data Exploration: How can we answer some of these questions? As advocated throughout this book, the best place to start is a thorough exploration of the data. Take a look at Figure 4.16. It shows four different scatterplots of the data. The top left panel shows a plot of the original data: salary vs. amount spent. What can we learn? We can learn that there appears to be a positive relationship between a customer's salary and his spending. However, the most striking observation is the "funnel" of the data cloud: for low levels of salary, there appears to be only a little variation in spending; however, as salary increases, so does the variation in the amount a customer spends. For instance, customers who earn $50,000 spend between $0 and $2,000; on the other hand, a customer who earns $100,000 can spend between $0 and $4,000. Why is this increasing variation in a customer's spending important? Because it implies that with increasing customer salary it gets increasingly difficult to accurately *predict* how much a customer will actually spend! Clearly, we would be more interested in the customers who earn more (because they have a higher potential to spend more). However, it is much harder to accurately predict the spending of a high earner than one with a much smaller salary.

Heteroscedasticity: So, what can we do to overcome the "funnel?" The funnel effect is often referred to as *heteroscedasticity*,[6] which means that the variability of a variable may depend on the magnitude of its values. Heteroscedasticity can often be "cured" by using an appropriate data transformation. The funnel shows that the variance of the data values grows with their magnitude. A logarithmic transformation often cures this problem – at least partially – because the logarithm has the nice property of making very large data values very small and, at the same time, leaving small data values almost unchanged. Take a look at the bottom left

---

[6]http://en.wikipedia.org/wiki/Heteroscedasticity.

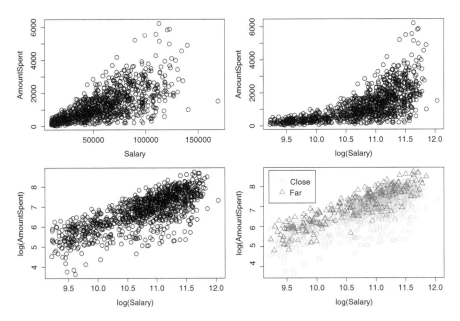

Fig. 4.16   Four different scatterplots of direct marketing data. The top left panel shows a plot of salary against amount spent; the remaining panels show plots of transformed data. The bottom right panel shows a plot of log(Salary) vs. log(Amount Spent) with different symbols differentiating between customers that live close or far.

panel of Figure 4.16. It shows a scatterplot for the same data, but we now plot both salary and amount spent on the log scale. We can see that the plot of log(Salary) vs. log(Amount Spent) no longer shows any funnel. In fact, it appears that it follows a very nice straight-line pattern. In other words, it appears very reasonable to apply a linear model to log(Salary) and log(Amount Spent).

Other Transformations: Not all transformations lead to the best result. Take a look at the top right panel of Figure 4.16. It shows the result of applying a log-transformation only to salary. We can see that transforming salary alone leads to a data pattern that does not look linear at all. (In fact, it appears as if log-transforming salary introduces *curvature* into the data.) Applying a linear model to this pattern would most likely lead to very misleading insight and wrong decisions.

Relationship with Location: The bottom right panel of Figure 4.16 shows the scatterplot of log(Salary) vs. log(Amount Spent), broken down by a customer's *location*. Triangles indicate customers who live far from a store selling similar items, while circles mark those customers who live near one. It appears as if the data pattern for far customers is somewhat different from those living close: the slope of the triangles appears to grow at a faster pace than that of the circles. How can we capture different data slopes in a regression model? Recalling Section 4.1, we can accomplish this with the help of appropriate dummy variables and interaction terms. We will discuss this in detail next.

```
Call:
lm(formula = AmountSpent ~ Salary)

Residuals:
     Min       1Q    Median       3Q      Max
-2179.67  -315.24   -53.51   279.71  3752.94

Coefficients:
              Estimate Std. Error t value Pr(>|t|)
(Intercept) -15.31783    45.37416  -0.338    0.736
Salary        0.02196     0.00071  30.930   <2e-16 ***
---
Signif. codes:  0 '***' 0.001 '**' 0.01 '*' 0.05 '.' 0.1 ' ' 1

Residual standard error: 687.1 on 998 degrees of freedom
Multiple R-squared: 0.4894,     Adjusted R-squared: 0.4889
F-statistic: 956.7 on 1 and 998 DF,  p-value: < 2.2e-16
```

Fig. 4.17 A simple regression model between salary and the amount spent. This model ignores all the patterns discovered in Figure 4.16.

A First Regression Model: We start out by discussing a model that *ignores* all the insight discovered in Figure 4.16. In some sense, this model would likely be the result of an analysis *without* any prior data exploration and thus shows how wrong we can go when ignoring patterns observed in the data. Figure 4.17 shows a regression model with amount spent as the response and salary as the predictor variable. Note that both salary and amount spent are *not* transformed, so it corresponds to the data pattern in the top left panel of Figure 4.16. From this model, we can learn that salary has a positive relationship with amount spent (as the coefficient equals 0.02196). But the most important aspect to take away from Figure 4.17 is the value of R-squared: it equals (only) 48.94%.

The log-log Model: Let's look at another regression model. Figure 4.18 shows the result for a model of log(Salary) vs. log(Amount Spent), so it corresponds to the bottom left panel of Figure 4.16. Compared with the model in Figure 4.17, we can see that it provides a much better fit to the data: the value of R-squared has now increased to 56.66%. Note that we accomplish this improvement of almost 8% by transforming only the pieces of information that enter the regression model (but without adding any additional variable to the model).

The log-Salary Only Model: It is also insightful to check what would have happened had we only transformed salary and left amount spent unchanged. Figure 4.19 shows the result of that model. We can see that the quality of that model is extremely poor: R-squared is only 44.71%, which is even lower than for the initial model in Figure 4.17. This illustrates that data transformations are not always beneficial. In fact, when applied in a hasty fashion, they can do more harm than good. The reason is that the transformation of salary alone has rendered a data pattern that exhibits curvature (see also the top right panel of Figure 4.16); it would

```
Call:
lm(formula = log(AmountSpent) ~ log(Salary))

Residuals:
     Min       1Q    Median       3Q      Max
-2.16381 -0.28005   0.07409  0.40193  1.11970

Coefficients:
             Estimate Std. Error t value Pr(>|t|)
(Intercept) -4.24279    0.29630  -14.32   <2e-16 ***
log(Salary)  1.02449    0.02751   37.24   <2e-16 ***
---
Signif. codes:  0 '***' 0.001 '**' 0.01 '*' 0.05 '.' 0.1 ' ' 1

Residual standard error: 0.5666 on 998 degrees of freedom
Multiple R-squared: 0.5816,     Adjusted R-squared: 0.5811
F-statistic:  1387 on 1 and 998 DF,  p-value: < 2.2e-16
```

Fig. 4.18 The log-log regression model; both salary and amount spent are log-transformed.

```
Call:
lm(formula = AmountSpent ~ log(Salary))

Residuals:
     Min       1Q    Median       3Q      Max
-1728.46  -442.07   -42.97   335.68  4129.92

Coefficients:
             Estimate Std. Error t value Pr(>|t|)
(Intercept) -9385.17    373.90  -25.10   <2e-16 ***
log(Salary)   986.07     34.71   28.41   <2e-16 ***
---
Signif. codes:  0 '***' 0.001 '**' 0.01 '*' 0.05 '.' 0.1 ' ' 1

Residual standard error: 715 on 998 degrees of freedom
Multiple R-squared: 0.4471,     Adjusted R-squared: 0.4465
F-statistic:   807 on 1 and 998 DF,  p-value: < 2.2e-16
```

Fig. 4.19 The effect of transforming only salary but leaving amount spent intact.

be very imprudent to apply a linear regression model to a data pattern with curvature, and the resulting R-squared value punishes us for this attempt.

Log-log Model with Location Dummy: By now we have established that a good way of modeling the relationship between salary and amount spent is by log-transforming both variables.[7] This implies that salary and a customer's spending

---

[7]In fact, we may even find better ways to model that relationship using alternative transformations, but given our efforts to this point, the log-log model appears like one of the better choices.

```
Call:
lm(formula = log(AmountSpent) ~ log(Salary) + Location)

Residuals:
    Min      1Q   Median      3Q     Max
-2.0336 -0.2708  0.0598  0.3380  1.1581

Coefficients:
             Estimate Std. Error t value Pr(>|t|)
(Intercept) -4.54246    0.27396  -16.58  <2e-16 ***
log(Salary)  1.03925    0.02537   40.96  <2e-16 ***
LocationFar  0.48632    0.03642   13.35  <2e-16 ***
---
Signif. codes:  0 '***' 0.001 '**' 0.01 '*' 0.05 '.' 0.1 ' ' 1

Residual standard error: 0.5221 on 997 degrees of freedom
Multiple R-squared: 0.645,      Adjusted R-squared: 0.6443
F-statistic: 905.9 on 2 and 997 DF,  p-value: < 2.2e-16
```

Fig. 4.20 The log-log model including a dummy variable for location.

are *not* related in a linear fashion. But what about location? How does a customer's location affect that relationship? We can investigate this question by creating a *dummy variable* for location. For instance, we can define

$$\text{LocationFar} = \begin{cases} 1, & \text{if location} = \text{"far"} \\ 0, & \text{otherwise} \end{cases} \qquad (4.31)$$

and subsequently including this dummy variable in our regression model. Figure 4.20 shows the results. We can see that including the location dummy adds additional quality to our model: the value of R-squared has increased again, and it now scores at 64.5%. This is another 8% improvement compared with the (already respectable) model in Figure 4.18. Or, put differently, location explains an additional 8% of the uncertainty in customer spending above and beyond the explanatory power of log(Salary).

Log-log Model with Location Dummy and Interaction Term: While the model in Figure 4.20 has shown yet additional improvement, we have not answered one of our initial questions: Does the rate of spending change with a customer's location? In addition, we have also detected two slightly different data patterns in the bottom right panel of Figure 4.16. Our last effort focuses on modeling these different data patterns.

Let Sal.Loc.Int denote the *interaction term* between log(Salary) and the location dummy. In other words, let

$$\text{Sal.Loc.Int} = \log(\text{Salary}) \times \text{LocationFar} \qquad (4.32)$$

```
Call:
lm(formula = log(AmountSpent) ~ log(Salary) + Location + Sal.Loc.Int)

Residuals:
     Min       1Q  Median       3Q      Max
 -2.0079  -0.2763  0.0589   0.3383   1.1043

Coefficients:
              Estimate Std. Error t value Pr(>|t|)
(Intercept)   -4.15586    0.32819 -12.663   <2e-16 ***
log(Salary)    1.00335    0.03042  32.984   <2e-16 ***
LocationFar   -0.76901    0.59027  -1.303   0.1929
Sal.Loc.Int    0.11703    0.05493   2.131   0.0334 *
---
Signif. codes:  0 '***' 0.001 '**' 0.01 '*' 0.05 '.' 0.1 ' ' 1

Residual standard error: 0.5212 on 996 degrees of freedom
Multiple R-squared: 0.6466,     Adjusted R-squared: 0.6456
F-statistic: 607.6 on 3 and 996 DF,  p-value: < 2.2e-16
```

Fig. 4.21 The log-log model with a dummy variable for location and an interaction term between the dummy variable and log(Salary).

We include this interaction term in the previous model. The result is shown in Figure 4.21. Our first observation is that the model has improved yet again; however, the improvement is only very small, as the value of R-squared now equals 64.66%, which is only slightly larger than the previous value of 64.5%. In other words, the inclusion of the interaction term does not add very much above and beyond the combined effect of log(Salary) and the location dummy. Moreover, we also note that in this new model the location dummy is insignificant (its p-value equals 0.1929) and the interaction term is also only borderline-significant (its p-value equals 0.0334). This brings up the question of whether the model in Figure 4.21 is any better than the one in Figure 4.20.

We can add yet another twist to our modeling efforts. Since the location dummy in Figure 4.21 is insignificant, we can remove it and rerun our model on the reduced set of variables. In other words, we now run a regression model with only log(Salary) and the interaction term. The result is shown in Figure 4.22. We can see that, by removing the location dummy, we reduce the overall quality of the model only minimally: the new value of R-squared equals 64.6%, which is only slightly lower than for the model in Figure 4.21 (which contains more variables and hence is a bit more complex); on the other hand, it is slightly larger than for the model in Figure 4.20 with only the location dummy but no interaction term.

The Best Model: We have seen that three models (in Figures 4.20, 4.21, and 4.22) are almost identical in terms of model fit. So which model should we choose for decision making? One of the basic rules of statistics is *parsimony*: given a set of (almost) equal models, we prefer the simpler (i.e., the one with fewer variables). This eliminates the model in Figure 4.21 (with both the location dummy and the

```
Call:
lm(formula = log(AmountSpent) ~ log(Salary) + Sal.Loc.Int)

Residuals:
     Min       1Q    Median       3Q       Max
-2.02281 -0.27601   0.05591  0.33717   1.13812

Coefficients:
             Estimate Std. Error t value Pr(>|t|)
(Intercept) -4.393589   0.272883  -16.10   <2e-16 ***
log(Salary)  1.025344   0.025313   40.51   <2e-16 ***
Sal.Loc.Int  0.045610   0.003384   13.48   <2e-16 ***
---
Signif. codes:  0 '***' 0.001 '**' 0.01 '*' 0.05 '.' 0.1 ' ' 1

Residual standard error: 0.5214 on 997 degrees of freedom
Multiple R-squared: 0.646,      Adjusted R-squared: 0.6453
F-statistic: 909.9 on 2 and 997 DF,  p-value: < 2.2e-16
```

Fig. 4.22 The log-log model with the interaction term between log(Salary) and the location dummy but *without* the actual location dummy.

interaction term). The decision between the remaining two models is not quite clear. Purists may argue that the last model (Figure 4.22) has a slightly higher value of R-squared and hence should be preferred. Other measures of model quality (which we have not explicitly discussed earlier) also point to this model: Figure 4.22 shows higher values of the *adjusted R-squared* and the *F-statistic* and lower values in terms of the *residual standard error* compared with the model in Figure 4.20. But there is one caveat to this model: due to the inclusion of the interaction term, it is a little more intricate to interpret. We will get to the interpretation next.

Interpretation of the Interaction Term: For the model in Figure 4.22, the coefficient of the interaction term equals 0.04561. What does this imply?

We start again by considering the case where the dummy variable equals zero (i.e., customers who live close). If the location dummy is zero, then the interaction term is also zero and all that remains is the coefficient of log(Salary); it equals 1.025344. Recall that both amount spent and salary are log-transformed, so this value needs to be interpreted in terms of its *spending elasticity*:

For customers who live close, every 1% increase in salary results in a 1.025344% increase in spending.

The insight above applies only to customers who live close to a store that sells similar items. How about those who live far away? For those customers, we set the location dummy equal to one (i.e., LocationFar $= 1$). This implies that the interaction term reduces to

$$0.045610 \times \log(\text{Salary}) \times 1$$

so the salary slope for customers who live far away adds up to

$$(1.025344 + 0.045610) = 1.070954.$$

In other words,

For customers who live far away, every 1% increase in salary results in a 1.070954% increase in spending, which is 0.04% higher than that of customers who live close.

This would be the correct interpretation for the model in Figure 4.22. We argued earlier that it provides a slightly better model fit (i.e., *R*-squared values) than the model in Figure 4.20. But is this slight improvement worth the extra effort necessary for the interpretation of the interaction term? An answer to this question can only be given on a case-by-case basis and will depend on the overall goals of the investigator (and, of course, also her familiarity with deriving knowledge and insight from interaction terms).

Lessons Learned:

- When we model data, we can apply several different ideas and concepts simultaneously. For instance, we can have dummy variables, interaction terms, and data transformations in the same model. By no means should we only think of these ideas as conceptually separated; in fact, we will derive the best models (and hence arrive at the most compelling decisions) when considering all of our modeling options simultaneously.
- In order to identify the appropriate data transformation or interaction term, data exploration is an absolute must. Scatterplots and data labeling reveal hidden aspects about data patterns. Without such careful examination, many important data patterns will remain hidden from us.
- When choosing between different models, we typically choose the model with the best fit. The model fit is gauged, for example, by the value of *R*-squared, but there are also additional measures such as adjusted *R*-squared, the *F*-statistic, or the residual standard error. For *R*-squared, adjusted *R*-squared, or the *F*-statistic, larger is better. On the other hand, smaller values indicate better models when it comes to the residual standard error.
- An additional consideration in choosing the best model is parsimony: all else being equal, we prefer simpler models (i.e., models with fewer variables). The reason is that simpler models are easier to interpret, communicate (e.g., to management or clients), and maintain. In fact, as we apply our model to understand future customers and markets, we have to worry about updating our model with new information. It is much easier to update a model if it is based on a smaller number of variables (as it is easier and more efficient to maintain the integrity of a small number of input variables).

- Another common consideration is the importance of individual predictors:
  if a model contains many insignificant predictors, then we often try to
  modify that model (or choose an alternate model). We can modify a model
  by dropping the insignificant predictors (and re-estimating it). On the other
  hand, given two models with the identical model fit (e.g., equal values of
  R-squared), we prefer the model with fewer insignificant variables. The
  rationale for this rule is as follows: Does it make much sense to pick
  a model when many of its components (i.e., variables) are statistically
  useless (i.e., insignificant)? The answer is "No," and hence we prefer
  models with a larger number of significant predictors.

Chapter 5
Data Modeling III – Making Models More Selective

In this chapter, we cover another important aspect of modeling: the danger of incorporating too much data. In fact, this point is a rather sensitive one: while too little information will not render a very powerful model, too much information can achieve quite the opposite effect – it can destroy the model's ability to give us any insight at all. Thus, much of our modeling efforts will be geared at achieving a fine balance between identifying just the right amount of data that is useful for our model and weeding out the information that does not carry any value. In other words, we want to make sure our models are selective and only admit information that is useful for the decision-making process.

5.1 Models with Too Many Predictors: Multicollinearity and Variable Selection

We are living in the information age, and it has become increasingly easy to collect and record information. In fact, someone records information about us each time we visit a Website or use a loyalty card. But is all this information useful for statistical modeling? Not necessarily. While the availability of information (i.e., data) is necessary for modeling, it is important to focus only on the *relevant* information. In fact, incorporating too much information into a regression model can render the model useless. Unfortunately, with the availability of terabytes of data in hundreds of data warehouses, filtering out the relevant information is as hard as finding the famous needle in a haystack. In the following, we discuss a few rather simple (but very effective) approaches for weeding out irrelevant information from our regression models.

Sales and Assets Data: Consider the data in Table 5.1. It shows information on profits, sales, and assets for a sample of Fortune 500 companies (recorded in millions of dollars). An analyst would be interested in using this data to better understand, for example, how sales and assets are linked to profits. In other words, do companies

W. Jank, *Business Analytics for Managers*, Use R!, DOI 10.1007/978-1-4614-0406-4_5,
© Springer Science+Business Media, LLC 2011

Table 5.1 Profits, sales, and assets (recorded in millions of dollars) for select Fortune 500 firms. See also file Sales-and-Assets.csv.

Profit	Sales	Assets
−6.8	2284.5	797.1
−78.3	2160.6	949.1
398.1	7554	3031.8
1508.5	53912.9	86971.6
134.5	9151.1	1575.1
118.1	22004.2	7398
43.4	2716.9	713.2
112	2771.9	1117.5
−925.2	2706.3	3020
117	5033.4	1116.8
−23.2	4639.1	1885.8

```
Call:
lm(formula = Profit ~ Sales + Assets)

Residuals:
    Min      1Q  Median      3Q     Max
-909.09  -39.15   30.83  117.77  316.85

Coefficients:
             Estimate Std. Error t value Pr(>|t|)
(Intercept) -88.156655 127.569747  -0.691    0.503
Sales         0.020070   0.020180   0.995    0.340
Assets        0.005871   0.012341   0.476    0.643

Residual standard error: 319.3 on 12 degrees of freedom
Multiple R-squared: 0.6385,     Adjusted R-squared: 0.5783
F-statistic:   10.6 on 2 and 12 DF,   p-value: 0.002231
```

Fig. 5.1 A first regression model for the sales and assets data from Table 5.1. The response is profit, and both sales and assets are included as predictors.

with higher sales (and/or assets) post higher earnings? And how can we derive the exact mathematical relationship between these three pieces of information from the data in Table 5.1?

Modeling the Sales and Assets Data: "What's the problem?" you may ask. After all, in previous sections we have already discussed in detail how to derive regression models from a set of data, and Table 5.1 has only three different pieces of information. So, how hard can it be to find a regression model for only three variables?

Figure 5.1 shows the estimated regression model with profit as the response variable and both sales and assets as predictors. That is, Figure 5.1 shows the estimated model for the relationship

$$\text{Profit} = a + b_1 \times \text{Sales} + b_2 \times \text{Assets}$$

```
Call:
lm(formula = Profit ~ Sales)

Residuals:
    Min      1Q  Median      3Q     Max
 -879.31  -25.10   57.02  125.48  306.25

Coefficients:
               Estimate Std. Error t value Pr(>|t|)
(Intercept) -1.249e+02   9.853e+01  -1.267 0.227313
Sales        2.918e-02   6.179e-03   4.722 0.000399 ***
---
Signif. codes:  0 '***' 0.001 '**' 0.01 '*' 0.05 '.' 0.1 ' ' 1

Residual standard error: 309.7 on 13 degrees of freedom
Multiple R-squared: 0.6317,     Adjusted R-squared: 0.6034
F-statistic:   22.3 on 1 and 13 DF,  p-value: 0.000399
```

Fig. 5.2 A model with only sales as the predictor.

We can make two surprising observations:

- *R-squared*: The value of R-squared equals 63.85%, which indicates that the model captures a large amount of the uncertainty in profits. In other words, sales and assets jointly account for over 63% of all the variability in profits. This is not bad, correct? While there may be additional factors that also affect a company's profitability, sales and assets seem to play an important role, as they capture almost two-thirds of all the possible variation in profits.
- *P-values*: The p-values for both sales and assets are very large (0.34 and 0.643, respectively). This indicates that neither sales nor assets are statistically important. In other words, while sales and assets jointly capture almost two-thirds of all the uncertainty in profits, individually – so it appears – both are useless!

So, what is going on? R-squared seems to indicate that the model (as a whole) has some value; the p-values, on the other hand, say that the individual model components (sales as well as assets) are useless. Is this a contradiction?

It gets even more confusing when we look at the contributions of each variable individually. Figures 5.2 and 5.3 show two additional regression models. Figure 5.2 shows a model in which we use only sales to predict profits (and leave out assets). Similarly, Figure 5.3 shows the effect of only assets on profits (ignoring the information in sales). We can make two additional observations:

- *Model with only sales*: Figure 5.2 shows that sales is an important predictor of profits. The p-value is very small and R-squared is reasonably large (63.17%).
- *Model with only assets*: On the other hand, Figure 5.3 shows that assets is also an important predictor of profits. Its p-value is very small and the value of R-squared is again reasonably large (60.87%).

```
Call:
lm(formula = Profit ~ Assets)

Residuals:
    Min       1Q   Median       3Q      Max
 -981.39   -41.00   -14.78    98.88   358.04

Coefficients:
              Estimate Std. Error t value Pr(>|t|)
(Intercept)   3.291274  88.390498   0.037   0.9709
Assets        0.017517   0.003895   4.497   0.0006 ***
---
Signif. codes:  0 '***' 0.001 '**' 0.01 '*' 0.05 '.' 0.1 ' ' 1

Residual standard error: 319.2 on 13 degrees of freedom
Multiple R-squared: 0.6087,     Adjusted R-squared: 0.5786
F-statistic: 20.22 on 1 and 13 DF,   p-value: 0.0006004
```

Fig. 5.3 A third regression model. This time, assets is the only predictor.

So, it gets more and more confusing: while the model in Figure 5.1 suggests that *neither* sales nor assets are useful for explaining profits, Figures 5.2 and 5.3 suggest that *both* sales and assets are useful.

Proper Interpretation of Regression Models: This is probably a good time to pause and briefly discuss a fine (but important) caveat of regression models. Regression models need to be interpreted very carefully. In fact, it is very important to distinguish between the information that *enters* a model and what is *left outside*. In the context of the sales and assets example, Figure 5.1 shows a model with *both* sales and assets; hence it measures the *joint* effect of these two variables. The joint effect of two variables may (or may not) be the same as their effects individually. Figures 5.2 and 5.3 measure only the *individual* effect of sales and assets, respectively. In other words, Figure 5.2 only quantifies the contribution of sales and completely ignores the effect of assets (and similarly for assets in Figure 5.3).

With that in mind, Figures 5.1–5.3 do not at all contradict each other. Figures 5.2 and 5.3 only claim that, individually, both sales and assets are useful for predicting profits. On the other hand, Figure 5.1 claims that, *jointly*, there is no use (i.e., there is not much use for a model that contains both variables simultaneously). Neither model contradicts the findings of the remaining models, so the only question that remains is with respect to the origin of the difference between the joint and individual effects of a set of variables. That is, how is it possible for the joint effect of two variables to be different from their individual contributions? The answer to this question is often referred to as *multicollinearity*.

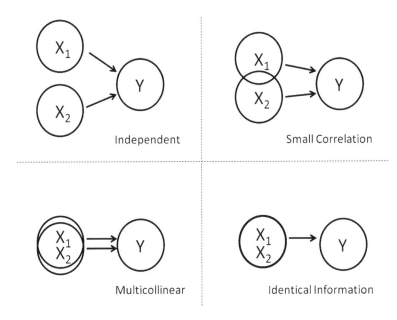

Fig. 5.4 Illustration of multicollinearity between predictors.

5.1.1 Multicollinearity

Multicollinearity refers to the situation where two (or more) predictors are (strongly) correlated. Consider the following (hypothetical) example. Consider a response variable Y and two potential predictor variables X_1 and X_2. Now, also assume that the *correlation* between X_1 and X_2 equals 1. Do you think that the following model is meaningful?

$$Y = a + b_1 \times X_1 + b_2 \times X_2 \tag{5.1}$$

The model in (5.1) does not make any sense at all. Since the correlation between X_1 and X_2 is one, both carry the identical information. So, incorporating X_2 into a model that already contains X_1 essentially amounts to *using the same information twice*. Using the same information twice is not only conceptually unappealing but also leads to grave mathematical problems.[1]

Figure 5.4 illustrates the concept of multicollinearity. In an ideal world, we would only want to include those predictors X_1 and X_2 in our regression model that are

---

[1] In regression, using two predictors with a correlation of one results in standard errors (and hence p-values) that are unreliable. The mathematical reason behind this is that the two predictors are linearly dependent in the design matrix, which, as a consequence, cannot be inverted. Matrix inversion is one of the core tools underlying the estimation of the regression model.

Table 5.2 Correlation table
for the predictors sales and
assets.

	Sales	Assets
Sales	1	0.9488454
Assets	0.9488454	1

- uncorrelated with one another (i.e., where the correlation between X_1 and X_2 equals zero) and
- highly correlated with the response (i.e., where both X_1 and X_2 have strong correlations with Y).

This is illustrated in the top left panel of Figure 5.4. Unfortunately, the ideal world hardly ever materializes in practice. In practice, we can get away with small dependencies among the predictor variables. In fact, regression still works alright if X_1 and X_2 feature a small correlation (top right panel in Figure 5.4). The stronger the correlation between X_1 and X_2, the more we should worry. The most extreme situation (i.e., a correlation equal to one; bottom right panel) hardly ever occurs, except for situations where we code the identical piece of information in two different ways. Examples are distances recorded in both inches (X_1) and centimeters (X_2), or weights recorded in both kilograms (X_1) and pounds (X_2). So, most of the time multicollinearity features a situation with two (or more) predictor variables X_1 and X_2 that have a very strong correlation but do not carry the exact same information (bottom left panel of Figure 5.4).

Diagnosing Multicollinearity: The previous discussion readily suggests diagnostic tools for multicollinearity. In fact, the most common tools for detecting this problem are

- correlation tables and
- scatterplots.

Indeed, Table 5.2 shows the correlation between sales and assets, and Figure 5.5 shows the corresponding scatterplot. Both indicate that sales and assets are highly multicollinear and should not be used in the same regression model *simultaneously*.

Cutoff Values for Multicollinearity: Your next question is probably "How high a correlation can we tolerate in a regression model?" Or, equivalently, "Is there a particular cutoff value above which we consider the correlation between two predictor variables too high?" Unfortunately, the answer is (at least in general) "No!" Unfortunately, there exists no single rule that universally applies and tells us when to include (and when to exclude) a predictor based on its correlation with other predictor variables. Surely, a correlation of 0.8 or 0.9 should always raise our concern. But sometimes a correlation of 0.6 between X_1 and X_2 may already be considered too high. The actual cutoff value, however, will often depend on the context. As one general rule, we typically scrutinize those variables most carefully that feature the *highest* correlations. In other words, if for a pair of variables the correlation is significantly higher than for all other pairs, then it is worthwhile to investigate the nature of their relationship more carefully (and, in some cases, take

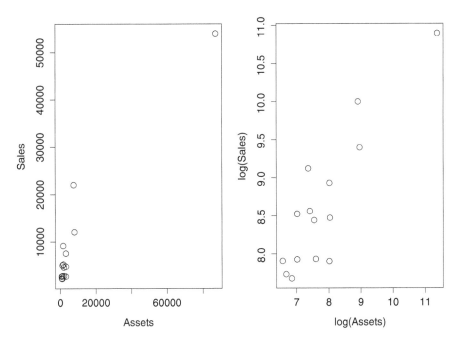

Fig. 5.5 Scatterplot between sales and assets (left panel) and log(Sales) and log(Assets) (right panel).

preventive action such as excluding one variable from the analysis). We will discuss more options for *curing* multicollinearity in the next subsection.

5.1.2   Curing Multicollinearity and Variable Selection

The cure for multicollinearity is, at least conceptually, very simple, and it is given by the very careful selection of variables that enter our regression model. However, in practice, we often face the challenge of hundreds or thousands of different candidate variables. While we could (and should!) run correlation tables and scatterplots for all possible pairs, this can be a daunting task. In addition, it does not provide us with any guidelines as to where we should best start with our modeling efforts. To that end, the concept of *stepwise regression* is introduced.

Stepwise Regression: "Stepwise regression" simply means that we should build our regression model in small, careful steps (rather than in large, uncontrollable chunks). Stepwise regression can be implemented in three different ways:

- *Forward selection*: We start with the smallest regression model possible (i.e., a model containing only one predictor) and then successively add predictors according to their relevance. We stop when we cannot identify any more relevant predictors.

	Forward Selection	Backward Selection
Start	X_1, or X_2, or,...., X_n	$X_1 + X_2 + ... + X_n$
Step 1	X_1	$X_1 + X_2 + ... + X_{n-1}$
Step 2	$X_1 + X_2$	$X_1 + X_2 + ... + X_{n-2}$
Step p	$X_1 + X_2 + ... + X_p$	$X_1 + X_2 + ... + X_{n-p}$

Fig. 5.6 Illustration of forward and backward selection.

A predictor's relevance is usually established according to measures such as:

- the strength of its *correlation* with the response, predictors with higher correlation being more relevant;
- its contribution to *R-squared*, predictors that add more to the value of *R*-squared being more relevant;
- its *significance* (i.e., the magnitude of its *p*-value), more significant predictors (i.e., predictors with lower *p*-values) being more relevant;
- its contribution to alternative measures of model fit – alternative measures include AIC or BIC and play a role similar to *R*-squared.

- *Backward selection*: Backward selection takes the opposite approach of forward selection. We start with the largest model possible (i.e., the model containing all predictor variables) and gradually remove individual predictors based on their lack of relevance. We stop when we cannot remove any more irrelevant predictors.
- *Forward and backward selection*: This is a combination of forward and backward selection. In each step, we allow a new variable to enter our model or an existing variable to leave.

Figure 5.6 illustrates the concept of forward and backward selection.

Stepwise Regression for the Sales and Assets Data: Figure 5.7 shows the result of stepwise regression for the sales and assets data in Table 5.1. The output is formatted a little differently from the model outputs seen previously, so we will focus first on explaining the information contained in Figure 5.7.

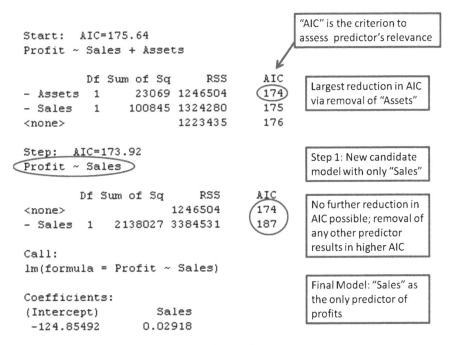

Fig. 5.7 Stepwise regression for the sales and assets data.

The first two lines ("Start") show the starting point of the stepwise regression procedure. We see that the procedure was initialized with both predictors, "Sales" and "Assets," entering the model. In other words, the procedure starts in a backward selection mode with the largest model possible. The next step must thus amount to removing one of the two predictors.

We can also see that "AIC = 175.64." AIC (which stands for the Akaike Information Criterion) is a measure of model fit very similar to R-squared. However, one main difference compared with R-squared is that *smaller values of AIC indicate better models*. Thus, since the initial model (including both sales and assets) has a value of AIC = 175.64, we will be looking for alternate models that reduce that value.

The next three lines in Figure 5.7 (starting with the column headers "Df," "Sum of Sq," "RSS," and "AIC") list different options for modifying our model. Since our initial model contains both sales and assets

$$\text{Profit} = a + b_1 \times \text{Sales} + b_2 \times \text{Assets} \qquad (5.2)$$

there are three different options. We could

- remove "Assets,"
- remove "Sales," or
- take no action; this is indicated by the term "none."

The result of any of these three actions is indicated on the right-hand side. In particular,

- removal of "Assets" will lead to AIC $= 174$,
- removal of "Sales" will lead to AIC $= 175$, and
- no action will lead to no change in AIC (i.e., AIC $= 176$).

Since smaller values of AIC denote better models, we should remove "Assets" from our model. Thus, the first step of our variable selection process has been successfully completed; the resulting model is of the form

$$\text{Profit} = a + b_1 \times \text{Sales} \tag{5.3}$$

The procedure now repeats the same process to see if any further variables can be removed or if any of the variables removed can be added back into the model. Thus, our next options are

- to take no action or
- to remove "Sales."

The result of either of these options is again shown on the right-hand side. We find that

- no action will lead to no change in AIC (i.e., AIC $= 174$) and
- removal of "Sales" will lead to AIC $= 187$.

Since an AIC of 187 is worse than one of 174, we should take no further action. And the procedure stops. The final model is thus

$$\text{Profit} = a + b_1 \times \text{Sales} \tag{5.4}$$

While the sales and assets data is almost too simple to justify applying stepwise regression, it illustrates the main points. In the next section, we discuss a more realistic (and complex) problem.

Lessons Learned:

- Models with too many predictors can cause problems. In fact, if some (or all) of the predictors are highly correlated with one another, then the results of regression analysis can be misleading. In particular, the resulting standard errors are unreliable and, as a consequence, we may no longer trust the p-values (and thus our conclusions about statistical usefulness). This phenomenon is often referred to as "multicollinearity."
- Multicollinearity occurs when predictor variables are (highly) correlated. Ideally, we want all the predictor variables to be independent from one another. However, in practice, this is hardly ever the case. One remedy for multicollinearity is the careful selection of predictor variables. In fact, we

only want to select those variables that are not too highly correlated with one another (but still have a strong relationship with the response).

- Variable selection can be done in different ways. If the data has only a small to moderate number of variables, then the selection of appropriate variables can often be done "by hand." To that end, it is helpful to inspect correlation tables and scatterplots.

- However, when the number of variables increases, manual selection is not only extremely burdensome but often impossible. There are automated algorithms that can help with the selection process. These algorithms are often referred to as "stepwise regression," which may include rules such as "forward selection" or "backward selection." While stepwise regression can automatically reduce the number of variables to a smaller, more manageable subset, it does not guarantee the optimal model. Only when used in conjunction with data exploration and domain knowledge will it lead to reasonable and valuable results.

5.2   Data Case: Using Variable Selection of Financial Indicators to Predict a Company's Stock Price

In this section, we discuss a more complex variable selection problem. Financial analysts and investors are often interested in understanding the relevance of accounting information in explaining (and predicting) stock returns. In particular, an analyst may be interested in determining how a company's profitability, liquidity, leverage, market share, size, or cash flow affect its market value. One problem with such an analysis is that there is often an abundance of accounting information available. In particular, besides information obtained directly from a company's financial statements, such as debt, cash, or revenues, analysts often compute *ratios* based on the information found in financial statements. These ratios could include profitability ratios such as gross margin or profit margin, liquidity ratios such as the current ratio or operating cash flow ratios, activity ratios such as asset turnover or stock turnover ratios, debt ratios such as debt-to-equity ratio or the debt service coverage ratio, market ratios such as earnings per share or enterprise value relative to net sales, and very many more indicators. The point is that financial information is plentiful. Moreover, financial ratios combine individual pieces of information from financial statements into new variables. As a result, many of the financial indicators and ratios are *correlated.* From a statistical point of view, this brings up problems of multicollinearity and, as a result, challenges with respect to smart variable selection.

Financial Ratios and Indicator Data: In the following, we discuss modeling of a set of data containing 25 different financial indicators and ratios. While modeling 25 variables already appears like a daunting task, the reality could be far more complex: financial information is plentiful; in fact, it is so plentiful that our data could have

Table 5.3 Financial indicators and ratios for a sample of 687 companies traded on US stock exchange. The data can be found in the file `Financial Indicators.csv`.

Type	Name	Description
Y	Stock Price	Value of the company's stock measured in US dollars
X	Total Debt	Cumulated value of debt
	Cash	Cash and marketable securities reported on the balance sheet
	Revenues	Income received from normal business activities
	Reinvestment Rate	(Net Capital Expenditures + Change in WC) / EBIT $(1-t)$
	ROE	Return on equity; net income / book value of equity
	ROC	Return on capital; after-tax operating income / book value of invested capital
	Net Margin	Net income / total revenues
	Invested Capital	Book value of equity + Book value of debt − Cash
	BVOfAssets	Book value of assets
	Net Income	(all revenue and gains) − (all expenses and losses)
	EBIT	Earnings before interest and taxes
	EBITDA	Earnings before interest, taxes, depreciation, and amortization
	FCFF	Free cash flow to firm
	CashPctOfFirmValue	Cash as percentage of firm value
	CashPctOfRevenues	Cash as percentage of revenues
	CashPctOfTotalAssets	Cash as percentage of total assets
	CapitalExpenditures	Cumulated capital spending
	Depreciation	Including both depreciation and amortization
	Trailing Revenues	Sum of a company's revenues over trailing 12 months
	TrailingNetIncome	Sum of a company's income over trailing 12 months
	IntangibleAssetsToTotalAssets	Intangible assets / total assets
	FixedAssetsToTotalAssets	Fixed assets / total assets
	DebtEquityRatio	Cumulated debt /Cumulated market value of equity
	DebtRatio	Cumulated value of debt / (value of debt + book value of equity)

contained hundreds or even thousands of variables. However, the following example will illustrate that 25 variables can already lead to quite significant challenges for the analyst. Table 5.3 lists the 25 different variables in our data.

Goal: Our goal is to find a model that can predict a company's stock price using information from its financial statements. In other words, we would like to find a model of the form

$$\text{Stock Price} = a + b_1 X_1 + b_2 X_2 + \cdots + b_k X_k \tag{5.5}$$

where X_i are some (or all) of the 24 predictors in the bottom of Table 5.3. A quick inspection of the variable descriptions suggests that many of the predictors may be highly correlated, so we are facing a potentially huge problem of multicollinearity.

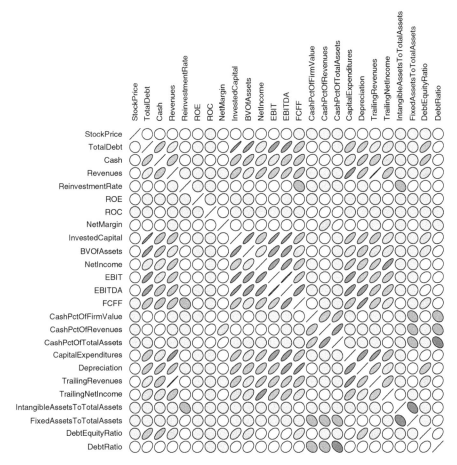

Fig. 5.8 A correlation graph for the 25 variables from Table 5.3. Colors and ellipsoidal shapes represent the sign and strength of the correlation. Blue colors indicate a positive correlation, while red colors stand for negative correlations. Similarly, upward-facing ellipses indicate a positive trend, while downward-facing ellipses indicate a negative trend. The closer the shape of the ellipse resembles that of a straight line, the closer the value of the correlation is to $+1$ or -1. Circles (in white) represent relationships of near-zero correlation.

Correlation Graph: A careful analyst will start with a cautious investigation of the variables' pairwise correlations. However, since we have a total of 25 different variables, the corresponding correlation table would have $25 \times 25 = 625$ entries – too many to be processed easily and conveniently. Thus we resort to a *visual representation* of the correlation table. Figure 5.8 shows a *correlation plot* for the 25 variables from Table 5.3. Colors and ellipsoidal shapes indicate the sign of the correlation – blue colors and upward-facing ellipses represent positive correlations; red colors and downward-facing ellipses indicate a negative correlation. A circle (colored in white) represents a correlation near zero. The darker the color (darker blue or darker red) and the tighter the ellipse, the stronger (i.e., closer to either $+1$ or -1) the correlation.

We can make several observations. First, it is interesting to note that the stock price has only a rather weak correlation with all of the financial variables – this will present a challenge for us in finding a good model. Moreover, we can see that there are many groups of variables that are highly correlated with one another. For instance, debt, cash, and revenue have a strong positive correlation with invested capital, the book value of assets, net income, EBIT, EBITDA, and FCFF. Moreover, the latter six variables are also highly correlated with one another (and so are debt, cash, and revenue). In fact, Figure 5.8 reveals that many of the 24 variables are highly correlated with one another. This is not too surprising since all of these variables come from a company's financial statements, either directly or in a derived form such as a ratio. The statistical challenge is to decide which of these variables is best to pick in order to predict stock price most accurately. For instance, since debt, cash, and revenue are highly correlated, we probably do not want to include all three in our model. But which one should we pick? Will debt provide a higher predictive power than cash? Or will revenue result in the best model? While we could (at least in principle) investigate all possible modeling options, we can generate millions of different models based on 24 different variables,[2] too many to be enumerated by hand. Hence, we will ask stepwise regression for help.

The Kitchen Sink Model: Before investigating stepwise regression, we first want to illustrate what could go wrong during a careless investigation of the data. Figure 5.9 shows the "kitchen sink" model (i.e., the model with all variables from Table 5.3). In fact, rather than carefully selecting appropriate and suitable variables from Table 5.3, we threw all of them at the model in a brute-force and ignorant fashion. While the "kitchen sink" model is a favorite approach among inexperienced students (and analysts!), it often does more harm than good.

Figure 5.9 shows that the "kitchen sink" approach results in a really poor model: R-squared is only 6.56%, so the model explains only roughly 6% of the variability in a company's stock price. Moreover, most of the predictors are statistically insignificant, as evidenced by the high p-values. Moreover, the row corresponding to the variable "Depreciation" shows "NA." In other words, regression did not produce any estimates at all for depreciation. The reason is that this variable is highly correlated with at least 12 other predictors. (See also the correlation plot in Figure 5.8.) In other words, the variable "Depreciation" is so highly multicollinear that regression breaks down and cannot produce any estimates. Seeing "NA" in your regression model should always serve as a red flag and cause you to carefully rethink your analysis.

---

[2]For a set of k different predictor variables, there exist 2^k possible models (ignoring all possible interaction terms), so, as we have 24 different variables in this case, there are as many as $2^{24} = 16,777,216$ different models!

```
Call:
lm(formula = StockPrice ~ TotalDebt + Cash + Revenues + ReinvestmentRate +
    ROE + ROC + NetMargin + InvestedCapital + BVOfAssets + NetIncome +
    EBIT + EBITDA + FCFF + CashPctOfFirmValue + CashPctOfRevenues +
    CashPctOfTotalAssets + CapitalExpenditures + Depreciation +
    TrailingRevenues + TrailingNetIncome + IntangibleAssetsToTotalAssets +
    FixedAssetsToTotalAssets + DebtEquityRatio + DebtRatio)

Residuals:
    Min      1Q  Median      3Q     Max
-41.600 -14.736  -4.820   7.733 721.840

Coefficients: (1 not defined because of singularities)
                               Estimate Std. Error t value Pr(>|t|)
(Intercept)                   4.370e+01  7.211e+00   6.060 2.28e-09 ***
TotalDebt                     7.523e-04  8.506e-04   0.884   0.3768
Cash                         -1.346e-03  1.946e-03  -0.691   0.4895
Revenues                     -1.217e-03  1.569e-03  -0.775   0.4384
ReinvestmentRate             -1.996e+00  4.443e+00  -0.449   0.6533
ROE                          -5.034e-01  7.836e-01  -0.642   0.5208
ROC                           1.276e-02  2.787e-02   0.458   0.6473
NetMargin                     1.472e+02  3.616e+01   4.071 5.25e-05 ***
InvestedCapital              -3.936e-04  6.516e-04  -0.604   0.5460
BVOfAssets                    3.615e-06  1.891e-04   0.019   0.9848
NetIncome                     5.294e-03  6.114e-03   0.866   0.3869
EBIT                         -1.432e-02  9.500e-03  -1.507   0.1322
EBITDA                        1.333e-02  8.718e-03   1.529   0.1269
FCFF                         -3.820e-03  3.284e-03  -1.163   0.2451
CashPctOfFirmValue           -4.459e+01  3.434e+01  -1.299   0.1946
CashPctOfRevenues            -3.210e+01  1.428e+01  -2.248   0.0249 *
CashPctOfTotalAssets          1.048e+01  2.861e+01   0.366   0.7142
CapitalExpenditures          -6.399e-03  6.392e-03  -1.001   0.3171
Depreciation                        NA         NA      NA       NA
TrailingRevenues              1.345e-03  1.445e-03   0.930   0.3525
TrailingNetIncome            -1.200e-04  1.645e-03  -0.073   0.9419
IntangibleAssetsToTotalAssets -2.060e+01  1.200e+01  -1.717   0.0864 .
FixedAssetsToTotalAssets     -1.943e+01  1.057e+01  -1.839   0.0664 .
DebtEquityRatio              -3.486e+00  4.913e+00  -0.709   0.4783
DebtRatio                     2.005e+00  9.691e+00   0.207   0.8361
---
Signif. codes:  0 '***' 0.001 '**' 0.01 '*' 0.05 '.' 0.1 ' ' 1

Residual standard error: 42.03 on 663 degrees of freedom
Multiple R-squared: 0.06563,    Adjusted R-squared: 0.03321
F-statistic: 2.025 on 23 and 663 DF,  p-value: 0.00325
```

Fig. 5.9 The "kitchen sink" model for the financial indicator data. The model contains all variables from Table 5.3 and illustrates what can go wrong when modeling data in a careless fashion.

Stepwise Regression: We now apply stepwise regression to our data. We want to caution that stepwise regression may not result in the absolutely best possible model.[3] However, the output of stepwise regression is usually a good place to start

---

[3]Stepwise regression is not an optimization method; it is a heuristic that systematically eliminates poor variable choices, but it does not guarantee the absolutely best possible model.

```
Start:  AIC=5160.16
StockPrice ~ TotalDebt + Cash + Revenues + ReinvestmentRate +
     ROE + ROC + NetMargin + InvestedCapital + BVOfAssets + NetIncome +
     EBIT + EBITDA + FCFF + CashPctOfFirmValue + CashPctOfRevenues +
     CashPctOfTotalAssets + CapitalExpenditures + Depreciation +
     TrailingRevenues + TrailingNetIncome + IntangibleAssetsToTotalAssets +
     FixedAssetsToTotalAssets + DebtEquityRatio + DebtRatio


Step:   AIC=5160.16
StockPrice ~ TotalDebt + Cash + Revenues + ReinvestmentRate +
     ROE + ROC + NetMargin + InvestedCapital + BVOfAssets + NetIncome +
     EBIT + EBITDA + FCFF + CashPctOfFirmValue + CashPctOfRevenues +
     CashPctOfTotalAssets + CapitalExpenditures + TrailingRevenues +
     TrailingNetIncome + IntangibleAssetsToTotalAssets + FixedAssetsToTotalAssets +
     DebtEquityRatio + DebtRatio
```

	Df	Sum of Sq	RSS	AIC
– BVOfAssets	1	1	1171291	5158
– TrailingNetIncome	1	9	1171300	5158
– DebtRatio	1	76	1171366	5158
– CashPctOfTotalAssets	1	237	1171528	5158
– ReinvestmentRate	1	357	1171647	5158
– ROC	1	370	1171661	5158
– InvestedCapital	1	645	1171935	5159
– ROE	1	729	1172020	5159
– Cash	1	845	1172135	5159
– DebtEquityRatio	1	889	1172180	5159
– Revenues	1	1062	1172353	5159
– NetIncome	1	1324	1172615	5159
– TotalDebt	1	1382	1172672	5159
– TrailingRevenues	1	1530	1172820	5159
– CapitalExpenditures	1	1771	1173061	5159
– FCFF	1	2391	1173681	5160
– CashPctOfFirmValue	1	2979	1174269	5160
<none>			1171290	5160
– EBIT	1	4014	1175305	5161
– EBITDA	1	4128	1175418	5161
– IntangibleAssetsToTotalAssets	1	5208	1176499	5161
– FixedAssetsToTotalAssets	1	5971	1177262	5162
– CashPctOfRevenues	1	8932	1180222	5163
– NetMargin	1	29274	1200565	5175

Largest reduction in AIC via removal of "BV of Assets" — stepwise regression removes that predictor in the first step

Fig. 5.10 First step of the stepwise regression procedure for the data in Table 5.3.

looking for even better models. In other words, we use stepwise regression as a *guide* (but not the final word) in our modeling efforts.

Figures 5.10 and 5.11 show the results of stepwise regression. The start of the procedure is shown in Figure 5.10. We can see that of all 24 different predictors, the removal of "BVofAssets" (book value of assets) results in the largest reduction in AIC (and hence the best model for this step). Thus, stepwise regression removes BVofAssets in the first step.

Stepwise regression computes an additional 16 steps (not shown here) until it stops. The result from the last step is shown in Figure 5.11. We can see that no further action ("none") results in the best model, and hence stepwise regression stops. The final model has seven different variables:

- FCFF
- CashPctOfRevenues

```
                              Df  Sum of Sq     RSS     AIC    "None" – best
<none>                                       1181084   5134   model is
- CashPctOfFirmValue           1      3529 1184613   5134   obtained by not
- IntangibleAssetsToTotalAssets 1      7824 1188908   5136   further adding
- FCFF                         1      7937 1189021   5136   or removing
- TrailingRevenues             1      8550 1189634   5137   any more
- FixedAssetsToTotalAssets     1     11038 1192122   5138   variables
- CashPctOfRevenues            1     11106 1192190   5138
- NetMargin                    1     39056 1220140   5154
```

```
Call:
lm(formula = StockPrice ~ NetMargin + FCFF + CashPctOfFirmValue +
```

```
Coefficients:                                          Final regression
              (Intercept)                NetMargin     model has 7
                4.488e+01                1.500e+02     variables.
                     FCFF       CashPctOfFirmValue
               -1.523e-03               -4.360e+01
         CashPctOfRevenues         TrailingRevenues
               -2.767e+01                2.252e-04
IntangibleAssetsToTotalAssets  FixedAssetsToTotalAssets
               -2.229e+01               -2.257e+01
```

Fig. 5.11 Last step and final results of the stepwise regression procedure for the data in Table 5.3.

- IntangibleAssetsToTotalAssets
- NetMargin
- CashPctOfFirmValue
- TrailingRevenues
- FixedAssetsToTotalAssets

Looking back at the correlation plot in Figure 5.8, we note that all seven variables have minimal to no correlation with one another, so stepwise regression has achieved one of its objectives by removing potential sources of multicollinearity.

The Value of R-Squared in Multiple Regression Models: But is the resulting model any good? Figure 5.12 shows details of that regression model. While almost all predictors are significant, we note that the value of R-squared is rather low (5.78%). In fact, it is lower than for the "kitchen sink" model in Figure 5.9. Why is the value of R-squared lower although we have (presumably) found a better model by eliminating multicollinear variables? The answer lies in one of the systematic shortcomings of R-squared as a measure of model quality: by design, *R-squared can never be reduced in value* when additional predictors are included. In other words, even if we include useless information in our regression model, R-squared will not decline. This explains why the "kitchen sink" model in Figure 5.9 has a higher R-squared although it contains a lot of collinear information. In fact, that model is so bad that some predictors (such as "Depreciation") cannot be estimated at all. Yet R-squared cannot flag this lack of quality. In short, R-squared can be misleading when comparing two models with different numbers of variables.

Alternate Measures of Model Fit: There exist alternate measures that cure some of the shortcomings of R-squared. One such measure is the so-called *adjusted*

```
Call:
lm(formula = StockPrice ~ NetMargin + FCFF + CashPctOfFirmValue +
    CashPctOfRevenues + TrailingRevenues + IntangibleAssetsToTotalAssets +
    FixedAssetsToTotalAssets)

Residuals:
    Min      1Q  Median      3Q     Max
-50.826 -15.314  -5.315   8.208 721.974

Coefficients:
                                Estimate Std. Error t value Pr(>|t|)
(Intercept)                    4.488e+01  5.657e+00   7.933 8.81e-15 ***
NetMargin                      1.500e+02  3.166e+01   4.738 2.62e-06 ***
FCFF                          -1.523e-03  7.128e-04  -2.136   0.0330 *
CashPctOfFirmValue            -4.360e+01  3.061e+01  -1.424   0.1548
CashPctOfRevenues             -2.767e+01  1.095e+01  -2.527   0.0117 *
TrailingRevenues               2.252e-04  1.016e-04   2.217   0.0269 *
IntangibleAssetsToTotalAssets -2.229e+01  1.051e+01  -2.121   0.0343 *
FixedAssetsToTotalAssets      -2.257e+01  8.958e+00  -2.519   0.0120 *
---
Signif. codes:  0 '***' 0.001 '**' 0.01 '*' 0.05 '.' 0.1 ' ' 1

Residual standard error: 41.71 on 679 degrees of freedom
Multiple R-squared: 0.05781,    Adjusted R-squared: 0.0481
F-statistic: 5.952 on 7 and 679 DF,  p-value: 9.733e-07
```

Fig. 5.12 Details of the final regression model resulting from the stepwise regression procedure.

R-squared. It is very similar in nature to *R*-squared; however, it penalizes the model for including useless information. Looking at the "kitchen sink" model in Figure 5.9, Adjusted *R*-squared equals 0.03321, which is lower (and thus worse) than for the stepwise regression model in Figure 5.12 (which has an adjusted *R*-squared value of 0.0481). Thus, adjusted *R*-squared picks up on the model's improvement due to the removal of collinear variables. A similar measure is the "residual standard error." The residual standard error measures the variability (or error) around the regression model, and we prefer models with a lower error. We can again see that the residual standard error in the "kitchen sink" model is slightly higher (42.03 vs. 41.71) – and thus worse – than for the model found by the stepwise regression procedure. A final way of comparing the two models is via the AIC. We argued earlier that lower values of AIC denote better models. The AIC corresponding to the "kitchen sink" model can be found at the initial stage of the stepwise regression procedure at the top of Figure 5.10; we can see that its value is 5160.16. On the other hand, the stepwise regression model in Figure 5.12 has an AIC value of only 5134 (see also Figure 5.11). Thus, by all alternative measures of model fit, the stepwise regression model is a better model.

Stepwise Regression and Model Assumptions: We have argued so far that

1. there are a lot of multicollinear variables in the data and
2. the model found by stepwise regression is (slightly) better than the "kitchen sink" model.

However, we have also noticed that while the model in Figure 5.12 is slightly better than the "kitchen sink" model in Figure 5.9, it is still very poor. Indeed, its R-squared value is only 5.78%, which implies that this model barely explains any of the uncertainty in stock prices at all. Can we improve the model's overall fit to the data? Yes, we can! However, in order to do so, we will need more than an automated procedure such as stepwise regression. In fact, we should go back to basic principles and carefully examine the patterns in the data. After all, stepwise regression *assumes* that the relationship between the input and output variables is linear. It is *your* responsibility to assure that this assumption is true!

Another Look at the Data Using Scatterplot Matrices: Figure 5.13 shows a *scatterplot matrix* for the seven variables in Figure 5.12. That is, it shows pairwise scatterplots and correlation values as well as histograms for the following variables:

- Stock price
- Net margin
- FCFF
- Cash as a percentage of firm value
- Cash as a percentage of revenues
- Trailing revenues
- Intangible assets to total assets
- Fixed assets to total assets

We can make the following observations:

- The histograms of the individual variables show that none of the distributions are symmetric; in fact, all variables are extremely right-skewed. This is not too surprising since most of the variables measure constructs that cannot be negative by design (e.g., a stock's price is never smaller than zero; a percentage – such as the cash as a percentage of firm value – can also never be negative). Moreover, it is quite common in business and financial data to find a few companies with extremely large values while most companies post average to moderate results. Both the combination of nonnegative measurement and few extreme outliers contributes to the generation of right-skewed distributions.
- The scatterplots between each pair of variables look extremely nonlinear. In fact, none of the pairs show a clear linear data pattern.

Recall that we have applied stepwise regression to the data above. Stepwise regression *assumes* that the input data follows linear trends. Looking at Figure 5.13, was it really justified to apply stepwise regression to this data? Or, should we rather have first *transformed* the data appropriately in order to render more linear relationships?

Log-transformed Data: Figure 5.14 shows the result of applying a logarithmic transformation to the data. In fact, it shows the same seven variables from Figure

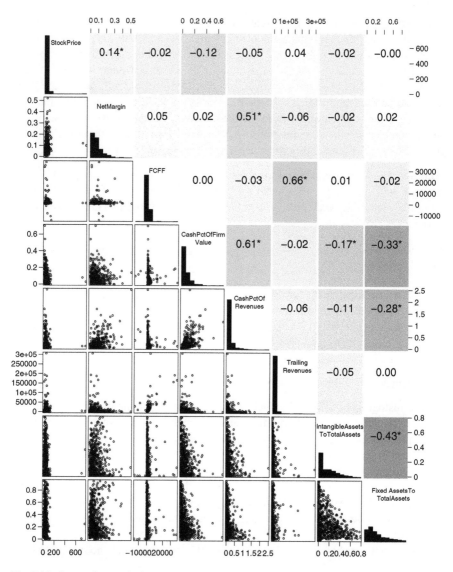

Fig. 5.13 Scatterplot matrix for the seven variables in Figure 5.12.

5.13; however, all variables have now been transformed to the log scale. We can make several observations:

- *Shape of Relationships*: The new scatterplots show that the shape of the relationship between many of the variables has improved greatly. In fact, many of the data patterns now resemble much more that of a linear trend. For instance, the relationship between log(Stock Price) and log(Net Margin) is much more linear than the corresponding data pattern in Figure 5.13. Similarly, the pattern between

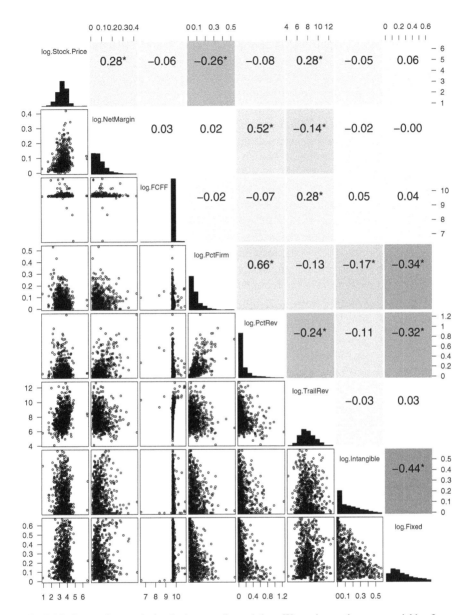

Fig. 5.14 Scatterplot matrix for the log-transformed data. We again see the seven variables from Figure 5.12, but all their values have now been transformed to the log scale.

log(Stock Price) and log(Trailing Revenues) shows a clear linear trend; this was not at all the case in the corresponding pattern in Figure 5.13.

- *Strength of Relationships*: We can make another curious observation: the correlation values suggest that many of the variable pairs now have a much stronger relationship. For instance, while the correlation between stock price and net margin previously equaled 0.14 (see the top row in Figure 5.13), the value for the log-transformed variables has increased to 0.28 (top row in Figure 5.14). In fact, glancing over the remaining correlation values, many of the log-transformed pairs post much stronger relationships.

Data Transformations and Correlation: Why does a simple transformation (such as a logarithmic transformation) result in increased correlation values? The answer is rather simple: the correlation (which is also known as *Pearson's correlation*) measures the strength of the *linear relationship* between two variables. That is, if there is a linear pattern, the correlation will tell you its magnitude. But the correlation only works for linear data patterns – if the pattern happens to be nonlinear, the correlation will not tell you much about the strength of that shape. In other words, if you apply the (linear) correlation measure to a nonlinear data pattern, don't be surprised if the resulting value is very small – all it tells you is that there is no linear pattern in the data you are looking at. But this does not mean that there is no relationship – the relationship is simply not linear! Thus, in order to derive the most value from the correlation measure, make sure you first transform your data appropriately!

Correlation Graph of Log-transformed Data: To bring the point across, we again plot the correlation graph from Figure 5.8, but this time we first transform *all 25 variables* to the log scale. The result is shown in Figure 5.15. We can see that many of the pairwise correlations have increased in strength. In particular, log(Stock Price) now shows a much stronger correlation with many of the predictor variables. We will see below that this also leads to a much improved model fit.

Stepwise Regression on the Log-transformed Data: We repeat the analysis from the beginning of this section, but we now apply it to the log-transformed data.[4] That is, we rerun stepwise regression on the log-transformed data. The procedure now takes ten steps to arrive at a final model. That model is shown in Figure 5.16. We can see that the model fit has improved tremendously. In fact, R-squared now has a value of 37.79%, which is a huge improvement over the value of 5.78% in the previous model (Figure 5.12). Moreover, we also notice that a larger number of variables now enter the final model (14 compared with only 7 previously). The reason is that the logarithmic transformation has rendered many of the relationships closer to a linear pattern; as a result, stepwise regression now recognizes the value of those variables and includes them in the final model.

---

[4] We transform all of the 25 variables to the logarithmic scale. The reason is that a close inspection reveals that every single variable shows a heavy right skew and patterns that are not linear at all, similar to the patterns observed in Figure 5.13. Hence we transform all of the variables from Table 5.3 to the log scale.

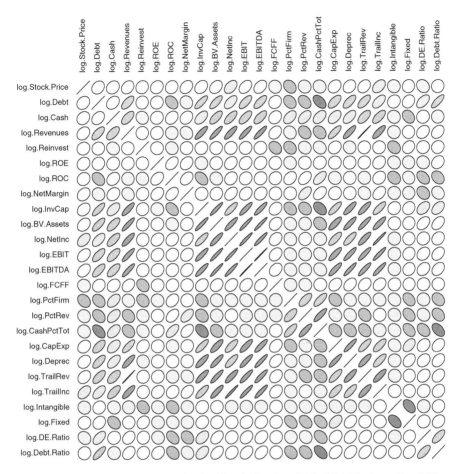

Fig. 5.15 Another correlation graph for the 25 variables from Table 5.3. This time, all variables have been transformed to the logarithmic scale.

Lessons Learned:

- Stepwise regression can help reduce a large number of variables. However, it does not guarantee that the final model has a good fit to the data; it only guarantees that the variables included in the final model do not post significant problems with respect to multicollinearity. The reason that stepwise regression does not guarantee the best data fit is that it assumes *linearity* between the response and all predictors. If in fact there exists a nonlinear relationship for some pairs of variables, stepwise regression cannot identify that pattern (or propose a remedy for it).

- To that end, stepwise regression does not replace data exploration or data transformations. In fact, stepwise regression *assumes* that the data entered into the model follows a linear pattern. It is our responsibility to assure

```
Call:
lm(formula = log.Stock.Price ~ log.Debt + log.Cash + log.Revenues +
    log.Reinvest + log.NetInc + log.EBIT + log.FCFF + log.PctFirm +
    log.PctRev + log.CapExp + log.Deprec + log.TrailRev + log.Intangible +
    log.DE.Ratio, data = log.data)

Residuals:
      Min        1Q     Median        3Q       Max
-1.9020059 -0.3039443  0.0004684  0.3201042  2.9164307

Coefficients:
                 Estimate Std. Error t value Pr(>|t|)
(Intercept)       7.25156    1.16077   6.247 7.42e-10 ***
log.Debt          0.04055    0.01191   3.405 0.000701 ***
log.Cash          0.05875    0.02334   2.517 0.012072 *
log.Revenues     -1.24881    0.23622  -5.287 1.69e-07 ***
log.Reinvest     -0.23976    0.13479  -1.779 0.075736 .
log.NetInc        0.13648    0.05422   2.517 0.012070 *
log.EBIT          0.15467    0.07875   1.964 0.049934 *
log.FCFF         -0.39162    0.11550  -3.391 0.000738 ***
log.PctFirm      -1.92490    0.47174  -4.080 5.04e-05 ***
log.PctRev       -0.40731    0.20742  -1.964 0.049972 *
log.CapExp       -0.04582    0.03145  -1.457 0.145604
log.Deprec       -0.10029    0.04219  -2.377 0.017718 *
log.TrailRev      1.14230    0.24030   4.754 2.44e-06 ***
log.Intangible   -0.57221    0.13686  -4.181 3.28e-05 ***
log.DE.Ratio     -0.52375    0.09071  -5.774 1.18e-08 ***
---
Signif. codes:  0 '***' 0.001 '**' 0.01 '*' 0.05 '.' 0.1 ' ' 1

Residual standard error: 0.4685 on 672 degrees of freedom
Multiple R-squared: 0.3779,     Adjusted R-squared: 0.365
F-statistic: 29.16 on 14 and 672 DF,  p-value: < 2.2e-16
```

Fig. 5.16 Stepwise regression for the log-transformed data. The model shows the result of stepwise regression applied to the log-transformed variables in Table 5.3.

that this actually is true. Thus, a smart application of stepwise regression first starts with a very careful exploration of the data and possible data transformations. Only once we are sure that all the patterns are close to linear should we apply stepwise regression.

- The output of stepwise regression is not necessarily the best possible model. Stepwise regression is not an optimization procedure that searches through all possible alternative models. Rather, it is a heuristic that applies a set of rules to the data. In general, this set of rules results in a model that performs *better* (i.e., is optimal in some sense), but it may not find the very best model among all possible combinations of variables. As such, we should not overly rely on stepwise regression. While we should use it as guidance to help arrive at a better model, we should also apply additional tools (such as data exploration and data transformation) and, of course, check the model's outcome against our expectations and prior knowledge.

Chapter 6
Data Modeling IV-Fine-Tuning Your Model

We have called this chapter "fine-tuning your model" because it covers a variety of concepts and methods that all share a common goal: to get more out of your model. Section 6.1 revisits the topic of model quality. Recall that we have already discussed the quality of a model in Chapter 3 (in Section 3.2.3, to be more precise). Why do we revisit the same topic again in this chapter? Because a model's quality depends on one's point of view. In Section 3.2.3, we have argued that a model is "good" if it explains a large portion of the uncertainty in the response variable or, in other words, if it explains many of the patterns observed in the data. However, since observed data is necessarily data from the past, our assessment of a model's quality has been retrospective until this point. But what about a model's ability to predict the future? A model that can explain the past very well does not necessarily predict the future equally well. In Section 6.1, we will thus revisit the topic of a model's quality and discuss the shortcomings of model fit statistics such as R-squared. We will also change our point of view and discuss ideas that can help us assess a model's ability to "look into the future."

Section 6.2 takes another look back at concepts discussed in previous chapters. In fact, that section revisits the idea of interaction terms and nonlinear regression models from Sections 4.1 and 4.2, respectively. Why do we also revisit concepts from these two sections? Because they are hard. More specifically, many realistic business relationships feature complex data patterns involving interactions among the variables and nonlinear data trends. We have seen in Sections 4.1 and 4.2 that capturing such complex relationships can be extremely hard and often requires a good amount of time-consuming (and sometimes frustrating) trial and error. Section 6.2 discusses two advanced regression methods that can alleviate the modeling task by discovering some of these data patterns in an automated and data-driven fashion.

We will start our discussion with the quality of a model.

W. Jank, *Business Analytics for Managers*, Use R!, DOI 10.1007/978-1-4614-0406-4_6,   125
© Springer Science+Business Media, LLC 2011

6.1   Assessing the Quality of a Model: Predictive Power vs. Model Fit

In this section, we discuss one of the most important aspects of modeling: how to best assess the true capabilities of a model. But what exactly do we mean by "capabilities"? Our answer typically depends on our objective. If our objective is to understand and explain patterns and trends from the past, then we will be looking for a model that can capture past events very well. However, most business decision makers are not so much interested in the past. This is not to say that the past does not matter. The past clearly matters, as we can often learn from events that occurred in the past. However, most managers would like to *predict the future.* For instance, we would like to know how many customers will buy our product during the next quarter, or how an investment will perform over the next year. Measuring a model's performance when capturing the past is very different from gauging its capability to predict the future.

Measuring a model's performance for capturing past events is relatively simple: since all the data that we collect is information from the past, we can simply use statistics that measure how close our model falls relative to the observed (past) data. We have already seen examples of such statistics, and they include R-squared, adjusted R-squared, or AIC. All of these statistics measure how well our model can explain patterns and trends from the past. Also, since these statistics measure how closely our model fits the observed data, we also refer to them as *model fit* statistics.

Measuring how well a model can predict the future is a significantly harder task. The main reason is that we simply cannot look into the future. Thus, since *we* cannot anticipate the future, how can we expect to gauge *our model*'s capability in doing so? The solution, though, is relatively simple. Researchers in the area of data mining and statistics have developed the concepts of a *training set* and a *test set*. Both sets are derived from the original data. However, we only use the training set to develop our model; then, we measure our model's performance on the test data. Note that while to us both sets of data are known, the model only "sees" the training data. Thus, from the model's point of view, the test data constitutes new (i.e., future) data. By measuring how well a model performs on the test data, we can get an idea of its ability to predict the future.

6.1.1   The Shortcomings of Model Fit Statistics

We first illustrate the shortcomings of model fit statistics in predicting the future. Recall that by "model fit statistics" we refer to measures such as R-squared, adjusted, R-squared, or AIC. Table 6.1 gives an overview of some of the most commonly used model fit statistics.

Table 6.1 Typical model fit statistics. All of these statistics measure how well the model explains patterns and trends from the past.

Name	Description
R-squared	Measures the proportion of the total uncertainty explained by the model
Adjusted *R*-squared	Similar to *R*-squared, but penalizes the model for too many useless predictors
Residual standard error	Measures how tightly the data fits around the regression line
AIC	*Akaike Information Criterion*; measures the overall fit of a model and penalizes it for too many useless predictors
BIC	*Bayesian Information Criterion*; similar to AIC, it also penalizes a model for using too much data

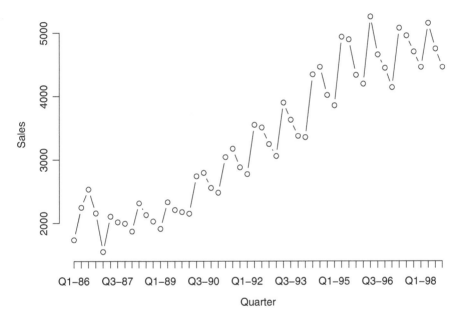

Fig. 6.1 The soft drink sales data from Table 2.7. The *X*-axis indicates the sales quarter (which ranges from Q1-86 to Q4-98), and the *Y*-axis shows the corresponding sales (measured in millions of dollars).

Model fit statistics measure how well a model tracks observed data. Since observed data is naturally data from the past, these statistics only measure a model's performance relative to past events. If the goal is to predict future events, model fit statistics may fail (or at the very least may lead to models that are suboptimal).

The Soft Drink Sales Data: Take, for example, the soft drink sales data from Section 2.3. (See also Table 2.7). Figure 6.1 shows a *time series plot* of that data for the quarters Q1-86 until Q4-98. Let's find a "good" model for that data.

Modeling the Soft Drink Sales Data: Looking at Figure 6.1, we can identify two patterns:

- an increasing *trend* over time (i.e., sales are increasing gradually from Q1-86 to Q4-98);
- systematic variation around this trend; in fact, sales consistently appear higher in the second and third quarters (Q2 and Q3) than in the first and fourth quarters (Q1 and Q4). In other words, sales appears to be *seasonal*.

How can we model these two patterns? An increasing trend over time simply means that with every additional quarter sales (at least on average) increase. Let t count the total number of quarters in our data. That is,

$$t = 1 \quad \text{for Q1-86}$$
$$t = 2 \quad \text{for Q2-86}$$
$$t = 3 \quad \text{for Q3-86}$$
$$t = 4 \quad \text{for Q4-86}$$
$$t = 5 \quad \text{for Q1-87}$$
$$t = 6 \quad \text{for Q2-87}$$
$$\cdots \quad \cdots$$
$$t = 49 \quad \text{for Q1-98}$$
$$t = 50 \quad \text{for Q2-98}$$
$$t = 51 \quad \text{for Q3-98}$$
$$t = 52 \quad \text{for Q4-98}$$

Since we have recorded every quarter between Q1-86 and Q4-98, we have a total of 52 quarters, and t ranges between 1 and 52.

How about the seasonality in Figure 6.1? If in fact the second and third quarters are always higher than the first and fourth quarters, then we can model this cyclical phenomenon with the help of *dummy variables*. Let

$$Q1 = \begin{cases} 1, & \text{if quarter} = 1 \\ 0, & \text{otherwise} \end{cases} \tag{6.1}$$

In other words, Q1 is a dummy variable for the first quarter; it equals one for every first quarter of a year and zero otherwise. Let's define dummies for the second and third quarters in similar fashion. A second-quarter dummy variable is

$$Q2 = \begin{cases} 1, & \text{if quarter} = 2 \\ 0, & \text{otherwise} \end{cases} \tag{6.2}$$

Table 6.2 The soft drink
sales data with a trend t and
three quarter dummies, Q1,
Q2, and Q3. Note that the
fourth row in the table has
Q1 = Q2 = Q3 = 0 – that
row corresponds to the fourth
quarter of '86. We hence need
no fourth dummy variable to
represent all four quarters.

Quarter	Sales	t	Q1	Q2	Q3
Q1-86	1734.83	1	1	0	0
Q2-86	2244.96	2	0	1	0
Q3-86	2533.80	3	0	0	1
Q4-86	2154.96	4	0	0	0
Q1-87	1547.82	5	1	0	0
Q2-87	2104.41	6	0	1	0
Q3-87	2014.36	7	0	0	1
Q4-87	1991.75	8	0	0	0

and in similar fashion we define a dummy variable for the third quarter as

$$Q3 = \begin{cases} 1, & \text{if quarter} = 3 \\ 0, & \text{otherwise} \end{cases} \tag{6.3}$$

Do we need an additional dummy variable for the fourth quarter? The answer is
"No." We can characterize the fourth quarter of every year as one in which

$$Q1 = Q2 = Q3 = 0 \tag{6.4}$$

That is, if the quarter is not the first (Q1 = 0), second (Q2 = 0), or third (Q3 = 0),
then it has to be – by default – the fourth quarter. We need no separate dummy
variable to characterize that quarter. A snapshot of this new data (including the trend
t and the three quarter dummies Q1, Q2, and Q3) is shown in Table 6.2.

A Regression Model with Trend and Seasonality: Let us now use the information
above to better understand sales. Consider the model

$$\text{Sales} = a + b_1 \times t + b_2 \times Q1 + b_3 \times Q2 + b_4 \times Q3 \tag{6.5}$$

The regression estimates corresponding to this model are shown in Figure 6.2.
  What does the model in Figure 6.2 imply? Using our knowledge from previous
chapters, we can make the following observations:

- *Model fit*: The value of R-squared is very high (0.939), which implies that almost
  94% of all the uncertainty in soft drink sales is explained by the model in equation
  (6.5). In fact, only 6% of the variability in sales is due to factors different from
  t, Q1, Q2, or Q3, which is quite remarkable since our model is rather simple and
  only contains factors pertaining to the temporal nature of the data. More evidence
  for the excellent model fit can be found in the large value of the adjusted R-
  squared (0.9338) and the small value of the residual standard error (286, which
  is small considering that the data is recorded in thousands).
- *Importance of individual predictors*: Looking at the p-values of the individual
  predictors, we notice that all but one predictor are highly significant. In fact,

```
Call:
lm(formula = Sales ~ t + Q1 + Q2 + Q3, data = train.data)

Residuals:
     Min      1Q  Median      3Q     Max
 -483.71 -153.81  -73.39  117.50  668.51

Coefficients:
             Estimate Std. Error t value Pr(>|t|)
(Intercept)  1332.88     108.61  12.273  2.9e-16 ***
t              68.75       2.65  25.945  < 2e-16 ***
Q1           -165.82     112.45  -1.475  0.14697
Q2            493.46     112.29   4.394  6.3e-05 ***
Q3            326.17     112.20   2.907  0.00555 **
---
Signif. codes:  0 '***' 0.001 '**' 0.01 '*' 0.05 '.' 0.1 ' ' 1

Residual standard error: 286 on 47 degrees of freedom
Multiple R-squared: 0.939,        Adjusted R-squared: 0.9338
F-statistic: 180.9 on 4 and 47 DF,  p-value: < 2.2e-16
```

Fig. 6.2 A regression model for the soft drink data. The model includes both trend and seasonality.

only Q1 has a rather large p-value and can hence be considered statistically insignificant. (We will get to a precise interpretation of this finding in a moment.)

- *Interpretation of the coefficients*: The interpretation of each individual coefficient needs a little extra care. Note that the value corresponding to the trend t equals 68.75. This implies that, when controlling for the effects of different seasons, sales increase by \$68.75 million in every quarter. In other words, *seasonally adjusted sales* grow by \$68.75 per quarter.

We pointed out above that Q1 is insignificant. What does this imply? Recall that dummy variables always perform pairwise comparisons. In this case, Q1 compares the effect of the first quarter with that of the baseline (which is the fourth quarter). Thus, the fact that Q1 is insignificant implies that sales in the first quarter – after accounting for the trend over time – are not statistically different from those in the fourth quarter. Or, put differently, *detrended sales* in the first and the fourth quarter of every year are the same.

We can interpret the impacts of Q2 and Q3 in very similar fashion. The coefficient of Q2 equals 493.46, which implies that *detrended sales in the second quarter exceed that of the fourth quarter by \$493.46 million.* And similarly, since the coefficient of Q3 equals 326.17, we can conclude that *detrended sales in the third quarter are \$326.17 million higher than the detrended sales in the fourth quarter.*

Quality of the Model: As pointed out earlier, this section is primarily about model quality. So, how would you characterize the quality of the model in Figure 6.2?

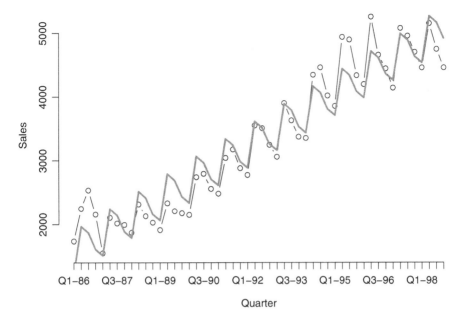

Fig. 6.3 Model fit for the soft drink sales data from Figure 6.1. The thick grey line shows the fit of the regression model in (6.5).

Most of you would probably conclude that this is a pretty good model. Why? Well, we have just concluded that the model fit is extremely high (R-squared near 94%); moreover, most of the predictors in the model are highly significant. So, what's not to like about this model?

The problem with all of the aforementioned statistics (R-squared, adjusted R-squared, p-values, etc.) is that they measure how well the model fits the observed data. Observed data is data from the past, so all that these statistics tell us is how well the model explains relationships from the past. A case in point is Figure 6.3, which illustrates the fit of the regression model in equation (6.5). The thick grey line corresponds to the regression model, overlaid on top of the time series plot of the observed data from Figure 6.1. We can see that the regression model tracks the observed sales data very closely, suggesting that it is capable of reproducing sales activity from the past very accurately.

But how well can the model *predict the future*? Assume that a sales manager wants to use this model to predict sales in the next year. That is, using the information from Q1-86 until Q4-98, he estimates the model in Figure 6.2. He then deploys the model to estimate the next four quarters; that is, to predict sales from Q1-99 until Q4-99. That data is shown in Table 6.3.[1]

---

[1]Of course, we would only have this information available *after* the end of that year. Here, we use it to illustrate the predictive capabilities of our regression model.

Table 6.3 Sales data for the
year 1999.

Quarter	Sales	t	Q1	Q2	Q3
Q1-99	4428	53	1	0	0
Q2-99	5379	54	0	1	0
Q3-99	5195	55	0	0	1
Q4-99	4803	56	0	0	0

Deploying the model to estimate sales between Q1-99 and Q4-99 amounts to plugging the appropriate values into equation (6.5). In order to estimate sales in Q1-99, we would calculate

$$\text{Sales}_{Q1-99} = 1332.88 + (68.75)(53) - (165.82)(1) + (493.46)(0) + (326.17)(0)$$
$$= 4810.65$$

because Q1-99 constitutes the $t = 53$rd quarter, and since it is the first quarter of a year, we set Q1 $= 1$ but Q2 $=$ Q3 $= 0$. In similar fashion, we obtain

$$\text{Sales}_{Q2-99} = 5538.69$$
$$\text{Sales}_{Q3-99} = 5440.14$$
$$\text{Sales}_{Q4-99} = 5182.72$$

Comparing these *predictions* with the *actual* values from Table 6.3, we can see that they are not identical. In fact, it appears as if the predicted values are *consistently* larger than the actual values. This notion is emphasized in Figure 6.4, which visually compares predicted and actual sales values.

Figure 6.4 suggests that our regression model severely and consistently *over-predicts* sales. In fact, Table 6.4 shows that our model overpredicts sales between Q1-99 and Q4-99 by over $1 billion! Thus, while the model fares very well in capturing sales trends from the *past*, it appears not as fit for predicting sales into the *future*.

6.1.2   Measuring the Predictive Power of a Model

Model fit statistics are not very suitable for capturing predictive performance because they are evaluated on observed (i.e., past) data. In an ideal world, we would obtain *data from the future* and evaluate our model on such future data. However, since the future is unknown to us, this is an impossible undertaking. So, what can we do instead? While we cannot generate any data that is future from our perspective, we can obtain data that constitutes the future *from the model's point of view*. In other words, we can obtain a set of data (from the past) and decide to let the model "see" only parts (but not all). To the model, the part of the data that it has not yet seen will then constitute future information. This technique of splitting the data into a part

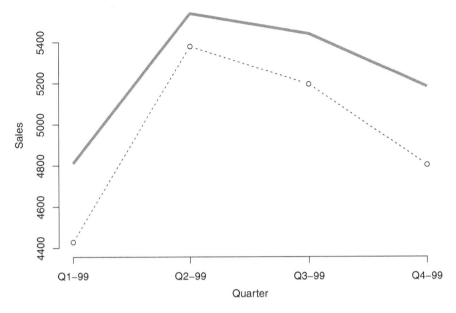

Fig. 6.4 Predicted vs. actual values. The thick grey line shows the predicted values for Q1-99 until Q4-99 based on the regression model in equation (6.5); the thin dashed line shows the actual values from Table 6.3.

Table 6.4 Prediction error for the regression model in Figure 6.2. We can see that it overpredicts sales by $1,167.20 million.

Actual	Predicted	Error
4428	4810.65	382.65
5379	5538.69	159.69
5195	5440.14	245.14
4803	5182.72	379.72
	Sum	**1,167.20**

that the model sees and another part that the model does not see is often referred to as generating a *training set* (i.e., the set of data that the model sees and that is used for model building) and a *test set*.[2] The test set will only be made available to the model *after* model building, and it is hence considered new (or future) data from the model's point of view. Table 6.5 summarizes the main features of training and test sets.

Generating Training and Test Sets: How can we best split a given set of data into training and test sets? There is obviously more than one way of partitioning a set of data. Most of the time, we prefer a *random* allocation. That is, we randomly

---

[2]The test set is also referred to as the *validation set*. In fact, some data miners use three different splits of the data: a training set for model building; a validation set for checking the model's performance and optimization of model parameters; and a test set for evaluating the final result. Here, we refer to test set and validation set interchangeably.

Table 6.5 The main features of training and test sets.

Name	Description
Training set	Is only used for model building; the models sees this set of data while determining the best data transformation and while determining which predictors to include in the model and which ones to eliminate.
Test set	Also referred to as the validation set. The model sees this set of data only after model building is finalized. The model's ability to predict cases in the test set is evaluated. The test set can be used to compare predictive capabilities across different models.

assign some cases to the training set and others to the test set. A random allocation has the advantage that it minimizes the chances of any systematic bias: since each case has the same chance of being selected, we are usually very confident that the test set has the same structural properties as the training set. What could happen if we did not select cases on a random basis? In that situation, the training set could have, for example, a predominance of male customers, while most of our female customers could be contained in the test set. The danger of such an approach is that the resulting model would probably be very good in predicting male purchase preferences but very poor at anticipating the needs of our female customers.

Training and test sets are typically generated in a random fashion. But how many cases should we allocate to the test set? Should we use a 50-50 split (i.e., allocate 50% of the data to the training set and 50% to the test set)? Or should we use a larger proportion of the data in the training (test) set? There is no clear-cut answer. It is quite common to use 70% or 80% of the data for the training set (i.e., to search for and find the best possible model), which leaves between 30% and 20% for the test set. Typically, we want to assure that we have "enough" data in the training set so that we can properly identify patterns and trends for our model. This is usually not an issue with data ranges in the thousands or millions. However, it becomes more tricky when we only have a few dozen rows of data. In that situation, careful selection of the right amount of data for the training set becomes important. One solution is the "cross-validation" approach, in which we select rather small test sets but select them repeatedly. In other words, we may only choose 10% of the data for the test set, but we select ten such test sets, essentially iterating once through the entire set of data. Most business situations, though, do not face this kind of problem since most sets of data collected during business transactions are often "awash" in information containing millions or billions of rows of data.

Splitting the House Price Data: Let us consider the house price data from Section 2.1. The data is shown in Table 2.1 and contains 128 "cases" (i.e., rows of data). While 128 rows of data is not an enormous amount of information, it is enough to apply the principles of a training and test set.

We apply a 70-30 split; that is, we reserve 70% of the data (70% of $128 = 90$ rows of data) for the training set and hence allocate 30% (or 38 rows of data) to the test set. We allocate rows in a random fashion in order to avoid systematic differences between the training and test sets. It is good practice to check the structural properties of each set and see whether their features coincide. Figure 6.5 shows a *scatterplot matrix* for all variables in the training set; Figure 6.6 shows the corresponding scatterplot matrix for the test set. We can see that while there are small (and expected) differences between the two sets of data, their main features are identical. For instance, in both sets of data, price is somewhat right-skewed and there is a slightly negative correlation between offer and price. While small differences exist, we can be confident that the test set is a good representation of the training set (and vice versa). We hence move on to using the two sets for modeling and identifying the best predictive model.

Modeling the House Price Data on the Training Set: Figure 6.7 shows a regression model for the house price data. This is the same model as in Figure 3.9 except that we now estimate it only on the training data. We can make the following (standard) observations:

- The value of R-squared equals 87.77%, which suggests that this model fits the (training) data very well. In addition, the value of adjusted R-squared is very high. All measures suggest a very good model fit.
- Many of the predictors are highly significant. In fact, only the North neighborhood is insignificant; this implies that home prices in the North are not significantly different from those in the East (the baseline). We also notice that the numbers of bedrooms and bathrooms are only barely significant. One possible explanation is the correlation with square footage: looking at Figure 6.5, we can see that the number of bedrooms shows a strong correlation with square footage (and so does the number of bathrooms). In other words, it appears as if, in the presence of square footage, bedrooms and bathrooms add only minimal extra value to the model.

We can summarize our observations in the following way. It appears as if the model in Figure 6.7 provides a very good fit to the data. However, there is also evidence that the model could potentially be further improved by removing some of the insignificant (or borderline-significant) predictors.

Evaluating the Model on the Test Set: But how well does this model predict the price of houses that will enter the market in the future? To answer that question, we apply the model to the test data. That is, for each house in the test data, we first estimate its *predicted price* using the model in Figure 6.7. We then compare the predicted price with the *true price*. In the following, we illustrate this process.

The first home in the test set is the home with ID #94. For this home, we have the following information on file:

1. Price $= \$157,100$
2. SqFt $= 2,080$

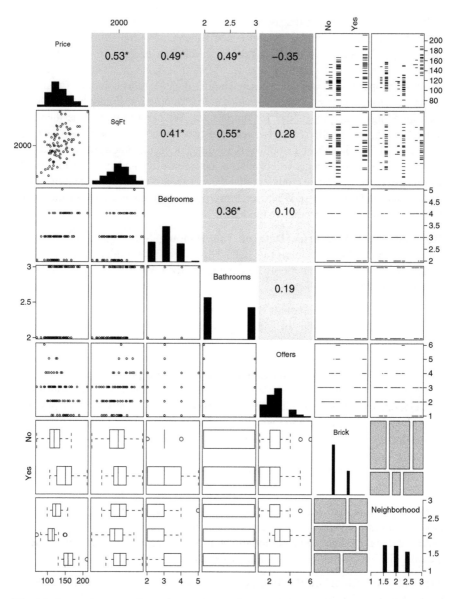

Fig. 6.5 Scatterplot matrix for all the variables in the training set.

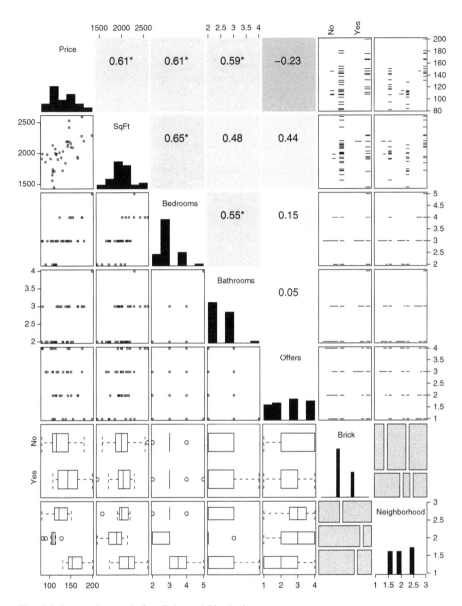

Fig. 6.6 Scatterplot matrix for all the variables in the test set.

```
Call:
lm(formula = Price ~ SqFt + Bedrooms + Bathrooms + Offers + Brick +
    Neighborhood, data  train.set)

Residuals:
    Min        1Q    Median        3Q       Max
-24183.9   -6963.3    104.3    6781.2   22179.7

Coefficients:
                      Estimate Std. Error  t value Pr(>|t|)
(Intercept)           7234.865  10968.233    0.660   0.5113
SqFt                    53.710      6.673    8.049 5.59e-12 ***
Bedrooms              3513.932   1829.676    1.921   0.0583 .
Bathrooms             4788.977   2564.197    1.868   0.0654 .
Offers               -8148.511   1323.610   -6.156 2.62e-08 ***
BrickYes             19025.220   2305.230    8.253 2.20e-12 ***
NeighborhoodNorth     1351.747   2811.397    0.481   0.6319
NeighborhoodWest     24516.912   3149.811    7.784 1.87e-11 ***
---
Signif. codes:  0 '***' 0.001 '**' 0.01 '*' 0.05 '.' 0.1 ' ' 1

Residual standard error: 9872 on 82 degrees of freedom
Multiple R-squared: 0.8777,      Adjusted R-squared: 0.8673
F-statistic: 84.08 on 7 and 82 DF,  p-value: < 2.2e-16
```

Fig. 6.7 Regression model for the house price data. The model is the same as in Figure 3.9 except that we now estimate it only on the training data.

3. # bedrooms $= 3$
4. # bathrooms $= 3$
5. # offers $= 2$
6. brick $=$ "no"
7. neighborhood $=$ "East"

Notice that $157,100 is this home's true selling price. Since the model has not "seen" this price yet, it constitutes a genuine prediction into the future from the model's point of view. We can generate the model's prediction by plugging items 2–7 into the model in Figure 6.7. This yields

$$
\begin{aligned}
\text{Predicted Price}_{\text{Home\#94}} = \ & 7234.865 + (53.710)(2080) + (3513.923)(3) \\
& + (4788.977)(3) - (8148.511)(2) + (19025.220)(0) \\
& + (1351.747)(0) + (24516.912)(0) \\
= \ & \$127,563.10.
\end{aligned}
\tag{6.6}
$$

Notice that we set the last three terms in equation (6.6) equal to zero since the corresponding dummy variables equal zero: home #94 is not brick, and it is located neither in the North nor in the West neighborhoods, so all three dummy variables assume the value of zero.

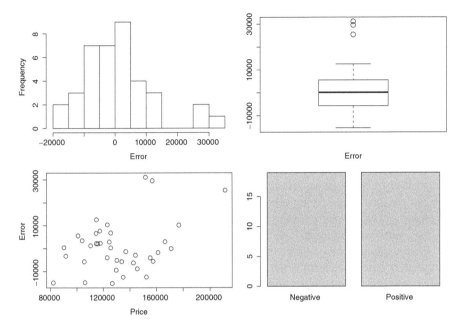

Fig. 6.8 Prediction error for the test set of the house price data.

Equation (6.6) shows that the *predicted price* for this home equals $127,563.10. This is quite different from its *true price* of $157,100. We can hence compute the *prediction error* as

$$\text{Error} = \$157{,}100 - \$127{,}563.10 = \$29{,}536.90 \tag{6.7}$$

In other words, our model *underpredicts* the home's selling price by almost $30,000.

Figure 6.8 shows summaries of the prediction error for all 38 houses in our test data. The histogram (top left) shows that the error is not quite symmetric: there are a few houses for which our model underpredicts the price by as much as $30,000 or more; a similar insight can be derived from the boxplot in the top right panel. The scatterplot (bottom left) between the error and the home's true price shows no discernable pattern; this suggests that our model's performance does not depend on the home's value.[3] The bottom right panel shows a frequency graph of the number of positive vs. negative errors; in our example, the model overpredicts as many times as it underpredicts, as the number of positive and negative errors both equal 19.

---

[3]But it may depend on other factors not shown here, such as the square footage or the number of bedrooms, or even other factors not considered in this data.

Table 6.6 RMSE and MEA
(computed on the test set) for
the house price data.

Error Type	Error Amount
RMSE	10837.48
MAE	7841.66

Root Mean Squared Error and Mean Absolute Error: While a visual representation of the prediction error is desirable (since it allows a very complete assessment of the model's performance), one often reports only one or two summary statistics. These statistics are referred to as the *root mean squared error* (RMSE) and the *mean absolute error* (MAE). In particular:

- The RMSE first squares all the individual error terms. By squaring errors, we treat positive errors in the same way as negative ones. In fact, one often has reason to believe that overprediction is as bad as underprediction. If that is the case, then squaring treats both errors in the same way. Next, we take the mean of all squared errors, which establishes the "average squared error." However, the average squared error is not measured in the same units as the original data. For instance, if price is recorded in dollars, then its squared error is recorded in "dollars squared." Squaring the units often makes no practical sense. Hence we take the square root of the mean squared error. This leads to the "root mean squared error" measure.
- The MAE has a motivation similar to the RMSE. However, rather than squaring the error terms, we take their absolute values. Again, the rationale is that negative errors are as bad as positive errors, and taking absolute values renders all error terms positive. Next we take the mean of all absolute errors. Since the units of the mean absolute error are the same as those of the original data, we need no further transformation.

Table 6.6 shows the values of RMSE and MAE for the house price data (computed on the test set). We can see that the error appears larger in terms of RMSE. The reason is that RMSE first squares all individual error terms. Squaring emphasizes larger errors and weighs them more heavily than smaller error values. Thus, data that contains many *outliers* is usually assessed better in terms of MAE (rather than RMSE).

Comparing the Predictive Performance with Alternate Models: Table 6.6 tells us the accuracy with which the model in Figure 6.7 predicts the sale prices of future homes. But is this the best possible model to predict house prices? Recall that both the number of bedrooms and number of bathrooms were borderline significant and did not appear to add much to the model. Could we obtain a better model by removing those two variables? Figure 6.9 shows the regression model with those two variables removed.

Does the model in Figure 6.9 provide better predictions of a home's future sales price? Table 6.7 provides an answer. It shows the values of RMSE and MAE for three different models: model 1 corresponds to the model from Figure 6.7; model 2 corresponds to the model from Figure 6.9; and model 3 denotes an alternate model in which we use only square footage to predict a home's price.

```
Call:
lm(formula = Price ~ SqFt + Offers + Brick + Neighborhood, data = train.set)

Residuals:
   Min    1Q Median    3Q    Max
-22872  -6954    747  6813  21358

Coefficients:
                   Estimate Std. Error t value Pr(>|t|)
(Intercept)       10385.697 11279.405   0.921    0.360
SqFt                 62.119     6.141  10.116 3.40e-16 ***
Offers            -7572.576  1339.428  -5.654 2.11e-07 ***
BrickYes          19757.148  2358.084   8.378 1.06e-12 ***
NeighborhoodNorth   284.074  2856.314   0.099    0.921
NeighborhoodWest  28695.971  2879.367   9.966 6.79e-16 ***
---
Signif. codes:  0 '***' 0.001 '**' 0.01 '*' 0.05 '.' 0.1 ' ' 1

Residual standard error: 10230 on 84 degrees of freedom
Multiple R-squared: 0.8655,    Adjusted R-squared: 0.8575
F-statistic: 108.1 on 5 and 84 DF,  p-value: < 2.2e-16
```

Fig. 6.9 A second regression model for the house price data. The model is again estimated only on the training data. Compared with the model in Figure 6.9, we now no longer consider the number of bathrooms and bedrooms.

Table 6.7 RMSE and MAE for three competing models. Model 1 denotes the model in Figure 6.7; model 2 denotes the model in Figure 6.9; and model 3 denotes a model with only square footage as the predictor.

Model	RMSE	MAE
Model 1	10,837.48	7841.66
Model 2	12,536.72	9345.93
Model 3	20,015.26	15,463.24

We can see that model 1 provides the best predictive accuracy – it has the lowest prediction error, in terms of both RMSE and MAE. The performance of model 2 is not quite as good: although we removed two barely significant variables, the prediction error increased. This fact illustrates a valuable lesson: statistical significance is not equivalent to predictive power. In other words, variables with low p-values do not necessarily add to the predictive power of a model. Looking back to Section 5.1, this further complicates our task of variable selection. In fact, while in Section 5.1 we only discussed variable selection with an eye on statistical significance and model fit, we could alternatively ask for a model that provides high predictive accuracy. As seen in the previous example, accomplishing both model fit and predictive power can sometimes be two quite contrasting objectives.

Lessons Learned:

- We can assess the quality of a regression model in two different ways: in terms of the model fit or in terms of its predictive power.
- Measures of model fit include R-squared, adjusted R-squared, and AIC. These measures assess how well the model recovers trends and patterns from the past. They do not tell us how well a model can predict future relationships.
- We can assess a model's predictive power via the concept of training and test data. The idea is to split the data into two disjoint sets. The model only "sees" the training data for model building. Thus, the test set acts as data from the future from the point of view of the model.
- While we find the best model using the training data, we evaluate it using the test data. We typically evaluate a model by computing the error between the true data value and the value predicted by our model. We summarize the errors by computing the root mean squared error or the mean absolute error – both measure the average error between the model and the truth.

6.2   Exploring and Modeling Complex Relationships: Nonparametric Regression and Regression Trees

Throughout this book, we have spent quite some effort making our regression models fit for capturing complex relationships. In fact, we have devoted the entire Chapter 4 to making models more flexible. Our efforts in that chapter revolved around the creation of dummy variables and interaction terms (Section 4.1) as well as data transformations using logarithmic or exponential functions (Section 4.2). While we have argued that all of these efforts pay off in the long run (i.e., via the discovery of a better regression model), they are involved and often require trial and error, which can be time-consuming. While we have also shown that exploratory graphs (such as scatterplots) often assist in the discovery process, they do not guarantee that we will find the best model and do not tell us precisely which data transformation or interaction term we should use.

All of this effort brings up a natural question: Wouldn't it be nice to have available tools that can discover such relationships *automatically*? In other words, rather than experimenting with different forms of interaction between two (or more) variables, wouldn't it be nice to have a method that can uncover interactions in the data (if they exist) in an automated fashion? And similarly, rather than sifting through dozens of scatterplots and trying out different forms of data transformation, wouldn't it be nice if there existed a method that could tell us quickly whether nonlinearities in the data really mattered?

You have probably answered "yes" to all of the questions above. And indeed there exist methods that can help us discover complex relationships in the data in a more automated fashion. In the following, we will discuss and illustrate two such methods. They go by the names of *nonparametric regression* and *regression trees*. Both methods are extensions of the basic regression model in that they share similarities with its principles – but allow much more flexibility in its execution. In fact, as with basic regression, both methods consider input and output (or target) variables, and we are interested in understanding how one or more input variables affect the target variable. But both methods are much more general (and less restrictive) in their approach. In fact, nonparametric regression does not assume any functional form between the input and the output. In particular, in contrast to linear regression, it does not assume any form of linearity. All that it requires is that there be *some* functional relationship between input and output, and it will try to approximate that function as well as possible. Similarly, regression trees do not make any assumptions about the functional form between input and output. In contrast to nonparametric regression, the method recursively partitions the data into smaller, more homogeneous subsegments. After segmenting the data in that fashion, it estimates a functional value for each data segment.

Nonparametric regression and regression trees have the appeal that they promise to automatically uncover nonlinearities and interactions in the data, respectively. However, no lunch is free. Indeed, the power of automatic discovery comes at a price. This price is usually in terms of *interpretability* of the resulting model. While we have spent many pages of this book interpreting the outcome of linear regression models, the insight that can be gleaned from nonparametric regression and regression trees is limited. For that reason, both methods are used more often in the context of *prediction* rather than explanation of past events; see also our discussion in Section 6.1 for more on this topic. While it would be unfair to say that they do not allow *any* insight into the relationship between response and predictors, they certainly do not produce insight as rich as the regression model from Chapter 3.

In the following, we discuss implementation and interpretation of both nonparametric regression and regression trees. We start out with regression trees which allow us to uncover complex interaction in the data in an automated fashion. After that, we discuss nonparametric regression, which could be regarded as an alternative (or rather a complement) to nonlinear regression methods, discussed in Section 4.2.

6.2.1 Uncovering Interactions with Regression Trees

A *regression tree* is a statistical method that develops a model in a hierarchical, tree-like fashion. It is very similar to a *decision tree*[4] in that it creates an *influence diagram* for our input and output variables. However, the main difference compared with decision trees is that a regression tree *estimates* such an influence diagram from the data (rather than developing it using – oftentimes subjective – decision analysis).

---

[4]See, for example, http://en.wikipedia.org/wiki/Decision_tree.

Due to the similarity they share with decision trees, regression trees are easily understood and – as a consequence – their insights are often easily communicated even to nonexperts.

From a statistical point of view, regression trees are especially intriguing because they promise to uncover complicated *interactions* in the data in an automated fashion. In Section 4.1, we have argued that interactions among individual variables often exist and that knowledge of their existence can make our models much more powerful. Take for instance the model in Figure 4.1 for the gender discrimination data: the inclusion of the interaction term between gender and experience rendered a model that provided a much better fit to the data and a much better explanation of the gender discrimination phenomenon. However, while the inclusion of an interaction term can result in a much improved model, *uncovering* the existence of such an interaction term is very hard in practice. In Section 4.1, we have argued that suitably formatted scatterplots can sometimes help unveil possible interactions, but scatterplots have to be custom-designed for each individual application and there exists no single graph that guarantees the discovery of every single interaction in the data. Moreover, interaction becomes harder and harder to "see" (i.e., via visual explorations) as the dimension increases; that is, as we move from two-way interactions (e.g., between gender and experience) to higher-dimensional interactions between three or more variables. Regression trees provide a way to explore and discover some of these interactions.

Back to the Gender Discrimination Example: Consider again the gender discrimination data from Table 4.1. We argued earlier that the rate at which each additional year of experience affects the increase in salary *depends* on the gender. In fact, male employees see a *faster* rate of salary increase (i.e., their salary goes up quicker for each additional year of experience) than female employees. We have thus concluded that the relationship between salary and experience is *moderated* by gender. In other words, there is an interaction between experience and gender and we hence include a corresponding *interaction term* in the regression model (see also the model in Figure 4.1).

Mosaic Plot of the Gender Discrimination Data: While the process of including an interaction term is a relatively easy one, it is much harder to *discover* the existence of such an interaction in the first place. In Section 4.1, we argued that a scatterplot such as in Figure 4.9 can assist in the discovery process. While scatterplots are very versatile tools, they are typically limited to visualizing three (sometimes four) different pieces of information at a time. In the following, we will explore the data in a slightly different way using the concept of *mosaic plots*.

Consider Table 6.8, which classifies the gender discrimination data according to salary, experience, and gender. For this table, we have recoded the information in salary and experience in a new way. For salary, we define the levels "high" and "low" as

$$\text{Salary} = \begin{cases} \text{High,} & \text{if salary larger than \$74,000} \\ \text{Low,} & \text{otherwise} \end{cases} \tag{6.8}$$

Table 6.8 Three-way
classification of the gender
discrimination data.

	Gender			
	Female		Male	
	Salary		Salary	
Experience	Low	High	Low	High
Low	42	21	22	20
High	37	40	4	22

And similarly for experience, we define "high" and "low" levels as

$$\text{Experience} = \begin{cases} \text{High,} & \text{if experience more than 10 years} \\ \text{Low,} & \text{otherwise} \end{cases} \tag{6.9}$$

We choose the cutoffs \$74,000 for salary and ten years for experience because they correspond to their *median* values.

Table 6.8 shows the corresponding breakdown. For instance, we can see that 42 female employees with low experience have a low salary. In contrast, only 22 male employees with low experience have a low salary. The numbers become more enlightening once we consider *relative frequencies*. Notice that there are many more female employees than male employees. (There are $42 + 21 + 37 + 40 = 140$ female employees but only $22 + 20 + 4 + 22 = 68$ male employees.) Out of all the female employees with *low experience* $(42 + 21 = 63)$, 42 – or 42/63 = 67% – have a low salary. In contrast, for all male employees with low experience $(22 + 20 = 42)$, only 22 (i.e., 22/42 = 52%) have a low salary. In other words, given employees with the same level of experience ("low" in this case), a significantly higher proportion of low salary earners are female.

The same holds true when we look at the high experience levels. In fact, the proportion of female employees with *high* experience and *low* salary is 37/77, or 48%. In contrast, the probability of a male employee with many years of experience but a low salary is significantly lower: only 4/22, or 15%.

Table 6.8 shows that the relationship between experience and salary is not the same for the different gender groups. That is, it shows that gender and experience *interact*. While that table contains all the information necessary to reach such a conclusion, it requires quite a careful interpretation of each number. In fact, a rushed observer may not necessarily "see" all the information and may not discover the presence of an interaction. To that end, it would be helpful to *visualize* the information in Table 6.8 in an insightful way. Figure 6.10 provides such a visualization, often referred to as a *mosaic plot*. The mosaic plot plots rectangles in sizes proportional to the underlying data. For instance, the overall size of all four rectangles pertaining to male employees (right panel) is much smaller than the overall size of all four female rectangles (left panel), emphasizing the difference between the numbers of male and female employees. Moreover, the small, thin rectangle pertaining to male employees with high experience and low salary (bottom left) quickly emphasizes that the relative proportion of male employees with high

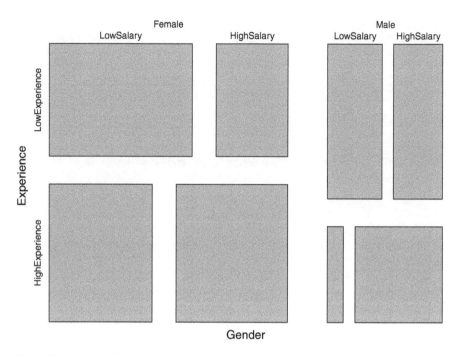

Fig. 6.10 A mosaic plot for the gender discrimination data. The corresponding values can be found in Table 6.8.

experience and low salary is much different from that of female employees, which once again suggests the prevalence of an interaction in the data. Yet, while the insight taken away from Figure 6.10 is the same as that from Table 6.8, the visual representation makes for a much quicker discovery of the data pattern.

A Regression Tree for the Gender Discrimination Data: Figure 6.10 suggests that we could understand the effect of gender discrimination by *partitioning* the data in the right way. Indeed, note that the assignment of "high" and "low" values to salary in equation (6.8) is nothing but a partitioning of the salary variable into two distinct values. In similar fashion, equation (6.9) partitions the experience variable into two distinct values. Table 6.8 then simply "counts" the number of occurrences for each combination of the partitioned data. For instance, it counts four employees that are partitioned as "Gender = Male," "Experience = High," and "Salary = Low."

But is the partitioning in Figure 6.10 *optimal*? In other words, have we found the *best* allocation into "low" and "high" salaries? Remember that in equation (6.8) we have chosen the cutoff value rather arbitrarily, simply by taking the median salary. Wouldn't it be possible that we could improve that cutoff in such a way that it would better distinguish between low and high earners? For example, would the mean (or the first quartile or the 80th percentile) result in a crisper segmentation? Moreover, why does Table 6.8 use *both* gender and experience to cross-classify salary? Why is experience an important component in this segmentation process? Note that in the generation of Table 6.8 we have never argued *why* it would be

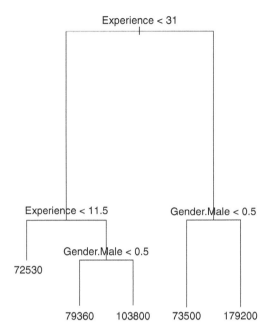

Fig. 6.11 A regression tree for the gender discrimination data. A tree consists of nodes and branches. The text above each node denotes the split decision. For instance, "Experience < 31" implies that if we follow the branch to the *left* of the node, we find all records with experience levels *less* than 31 years; on the other hand, following the branch to the *right*, we find employees with more than 31 years of experience. Reading a node for binary or categorical variables requires extra care. For instance, the node "Gender.Male < 0.5" implies that to the left we find employees with gender "less than 0.5." Since gender only assumes the values 0 = (female) and 1 = (male), a value of less than 0.5 must refer to female employees. The terminal node (at the bottom of the tree) denotes the average salary for that segment. Regression trees are best understood by following a terminal node "backward" up in the tree. For instance, 179,200 at the bottom right implies that for employees who are male ("Gender.Male > 0.5") and who have more than 31 years of experience ("Experience > 31"), the average salary equals $179,200. On the other hand, the adjacent terminal node 73,500 implies that for female employees ("Gender.Male < 0.5") who have more than 31 years of experience, the average salary equals only $73,500.

necessary to include experience – we have simply made an arbitrary decision to include that variable no matter what.

So, to summarize, the partitioning in Figure 6.10 is a valid segmentation of the data. But it is also an arbitrary one. Neither the segmentation variables nor their cutoff values have been chosen in an "optimal" fashion. While there could be more than one way to define "optimality," Figure 6.10 does not make a reference to any. Is there a method that could both detect the best set of variables to include in the segmentation process and compute their optimal cutoff value? The answer is "yes," and it can be found in the form of *regression trees*.

Figure 6.11 shows a regression tree for the gender discrimination data. Recall that we have three different variables: gender, experience, and salary. In fact, the goal is to understand how gender and/or experience (the input variables) can explain an employee's salary (the output or target variable). In contrast to mosaic plots, a regression tree differentiates between input and output variables. In fact, it operates in a fashion quite similar to regression models in that we would like to use a set of input variables to explain or predict a target variable.

A regression tree consists of branches and nodes. The "terminal nodes" (i.e., the nodes at the bottom of the tree) display estimates for the target variable. In the case of Figure 6.11, we can identify five terminal nodes, with values of 72,530, 79,360, 103,800, 73,500, and 179,200. These five values denote estimated values of salary. The only question that remains is how these salary values are linked to the two input variables, gender and experience.

In order to understand the relationship between input and target variables, we start at the top of the tree. The very first node has the label "Experience < 31." Labels denote splitting decisions. In the case of the first node, if we follow the branch to the left of the node, we will encounter only employees with *less than 31 years of experience.* In contrast, the branch to the right contains only records for employees with *not* less than 31 years of experience; that is, employees with 31 or more years of experience.

Let us follow the branch from the first node to the left. The next node is labeled "Experience < 11.5." If we follow its branch to the left, we arrive at a terminal node labeled "72,530." Thus, we can interpret this in the following way: employees who have less than 31 years of experience (first node to the left) *and* less than 11.5 years of experience (second node to the left) can expect an average salary of $72,530. Or, put differently, since less than 11.5 years of experience is a stricter condition than less than 31 years of experience, employees with less than 11.5 years of experience can expect an average salary of $72,530. Notice that this particular result is independent of gender since we did not encounter any gender node in the leftmost path of the tree.

Gender enters the result for all other terminal nodes. In fact, the second terminal node from the left reads "79,360." If we move up its branch to the nearest node, we can find a label "Gender.Male < 0.5." Gender is a categorical variable, and we re-coded its dummy variable Gender.Male to assume the value 1 for male employees and 0 for female employees. Thus "Gender.Male < 0.5" must refer to all female employees. We can thus interpret the final node "79,360" as the average salary for female employees (left of "Gender.Male < 0.5") with more than 11.5 years of experience (right of "Experience < 11.5") but less than 31 years of experience (left of "Experience < 31"). In other words, female employees with more than 11.5 but less than 31 years of experience can expect to earn, on average, $79,360.

We can apply a similar rationale to make sense of the remaining terminal nodes. The third node from the left ("103,800") implies that male employees (right of "Gender.Male < 0.5") with more than 11.5 but less than 31 years of experience can expect to earn $103,800 on average – over $24,000 more than their female colleagues with the exact same experience level. This is also the first indication the tree gives us about a potential interaction between gender and experience: despite the same level of experience, earnings of males are significantly different from those of females.

The fourth terminal node reads "73,500." Following arguments similar to those above, it implies that female employees with *more than 31 years* of experience make, on average, $73,500. This is again significantly lower than the value of the fifth node ("179,200"): that node implies that male employees with the same qualifications can expect earnings of $179,200 on average – over $100,000 more than their female counterparts. So, our findings imply that the impact of experience is not only moderated by gender; its effect increases for higher levels of experience. While the gender difference in salary is only $24,000 for lower levels of experience, it increases to over $100,000 for high experience levels. Thus, the regression tree suggests that there is not only an interaction between gender and experience but that the form and nature of this interaction may be far more complex than what our linear regression model in Figure 4.8 is able to capture. Below, we will explore whether the regression tree is in fact superior in capturing this interaction compared with the linear regression model.

Investigating the Predictive Accuracy of the Regression Tree: We have argued that the regression tree in Figure 6.11 can help unveil complicated interactions in the data. But is this model "any good?" In particular, how well does it anticipate the salary of a future employee? In other words, how does the model fare in terms of its predictive accuracy? Note that we are particularly interested in investigating the tree's predictive accuracy (more than its data fit) since regression trees have a tendency to fit the observed data very closely. That is, sometimes regression trees trace the observed data too closely (they "overfit"), which brings up questions with respect their the generalizability to events outside the data. To that end, we investigate the tree's predictive accuracy.

Similar to the steps outlined in Section 6.1, we first split the data into a training set and a test set. We again choose to reserve 70% of the data (or 146 rows) for the training set, which leaves 30% (or 62 rows of data) for the test set. We again allocate data in random fashion to each of the two sets. Figure 6.12 shows the distribution of salary for each of the two sets of data. We can see that the test set mimics the shape of salary in the training set. In particular, while the training set contains a few more extreme salary values, both distributions feature a clear right skew.

We compare the regression tree in Figure 6.11 with all three regression models from Section 4.1. That is, we first compare it against a model that features only experience as predictor

$$\text{Model 1:   Salary} = a + b_1 \times \text{Experience} \qquad (6.10)$$

as in Figure 4.4. We also compare it against a model with both experience and the gender dummy, as in Figure 4.6;

$$\text{Model 2:   Salary} = a + b_1 \times \text{Experience} + b_2 \times \text{Gender.Male} \qquad (6.11)$$

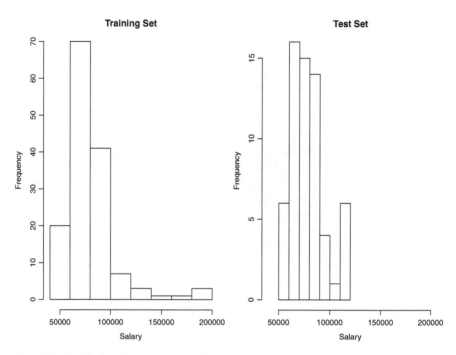

Fig. 6.12 Distribution of salary in the training set (left panel) and the test set (right panel).

And finally, we estimate a third model with both the gender dummy and the interaction term between experience and gender. That is, we replicate the model from Figure 4.8:

$$\text{Model 3: Salary} = a + b_1 \times \text{Experience} + b_2 \times \text{Gender.Male} + b_3 \times \text{Gender.Exp.Int} \tag{6.12}$$

We refer to these models as Models 1–3. The only difference compared with the models estimated in Section 4.1 is that Models 1–3 are estimated only on the *training set*; we will subsequently compare their performance on the *test set*.

Table 6.9 shows the performance of the regression tree relative to Models 1–3 for the test set. We again report the *root mean squared error* (RMSE) as well as the *mean absolute error* (MAE). Recall that smaller error values indicate better models. We can see that the regression tree (first line) has the smallest error, both in terms of RMSE and MAE. This suggests that the tree not only captures complex interactions in the observed data but also results in a model that generalizes well to new (and future) observations. It is also curious to note that Model 3 features the worst performance (at least in terms of RMSE). Going back to that model's estimates in Figure 4.8, we recall that Model 3 featured the *highest value of R-squared*, higher than the values in Figure 4.4 and Figure 4.6. Thus, while the regression model with the interaction term provides a good fit to the observed (i.e., past) data, it appears not as capable of predicting the outcome of future interactions.

Table 6.9 RMSE and MAE
for the regression tree
compared with three linear
models, 1–3.

Model	RMSE	MAE
Tree	14317.00	10831.66
Model 1	15774.26	12750.03
Model 2	16510.53	13047.51
Model 3	17692.47	12479.21

There are a few important takeaways from Table 6.9. First, the results suggest that the regression tree is superior, at least in terms of its predictive capabilities. We are quick to point out that this is not necessarily a general rule. In fact, there are many examples in the academic literature as well as from industry practice where a regression tree *overfits* the data and hence does not provide good generalizability to future events. Thus, the regression tree is not a cure for all evils; it still requires a very careful evaluation against all other possible options. The second takeaway is that models may look very good in terms of their model fit but perform poorly when it comes to predictive power. A case in point is the performance of the linear regression model with the interaction term (Model 3). While it has a very high R-squared value (and hence a good fit), its capability to anticipate the future is rather limited. Does that mean that we have to automatically dismiss this model? Not necessarily. The choice of our model (and consequently the choice of our evaluation criterion) depends on our objective. There are plenty of examples where a good model fit is more desirable than excellent prediction. One example would be a courtroom setting in which a judge needs to decide whether a company has performed systematic discrimination *in the past*. In that situation, the main objective would be to better understand events from the past, and hence we would be looking for models with high values of R-squared (rather than small prediction errors). In other words, as our objectives change, so will our evaluation criteria – and with them the choice of our model.

Lessons Learned:

- Regression trees are an alternate approach to statistical modeling. Trees partition the data in a recursive fashion, identifying the best variables for data segmentation as well as the best cutoff values to perform a data split.
- One of the main appeals of regression trees is that they explore the data and may unveil complex interactions in an automated fashion. That is, in contrast to interaction terms in linear regression models, no interaction variables have to be defined and explicitly included in the model. Rather, the regression tree will automatically identify such interactions if they are prevalent in the data.
- Regression trees need careful interpretation in terms of their branches and nodes. In particular, the variable of interest (the target variable) is usually found in the terminal node at the bottom of the tree. Moving back up from the terminal node to the top of the tree, we can understand the relationships between input and output variables.

- Regression trees have a tendency to fit the data very closely, sometimes too close. In other words, they may overfit the data, which results in poor generalizability of the result to other (or future) situations and scenarios. To that end, investigating and comparing the tree in terms of its predictive capability is good practice. The predictive capability can be assessed using the concepts of a training set and a test set.
- Regression trees may not always result in the best model. Their performance is best compared against a set of alternate models (such as standard linear regression models).

6.2.2   Modeling Nonlinear Relationships Using Nonparametric Regression

We have argued in Section 4.2 that it is quite common to find business processes that do not behave in a linear fashion. One example is the law of *diminishing returns*, in which each additional unit of variable input yields smaller and smaller increases in output. We have previously referred to the example of sales and advertising, which may quite often be subject to this law: while more advertising often results in higher sales, one may encounter a point beyond which additional advertising expenditures result in a marginal *decrease* in sales. Of course, there may also be situations where quite the opposite is true (i.e., where a law of *accelerating returns* holds): we have seen that, in the gender discrimination example in Section 4.1, male salaries appear to be growing *faster* with increasing levels of experience (see also Figure 4.10). Additional examples of nonlinear effects commonly found in business processes are the *learning curve effect*, in which the increase in retention of information is sharpest after some initial attempts and then gradually evens out, or *Moore's Law*, which states that the number of transistors that can be placed inexpensively on an integrated circuit doubles approximately every two years (i.e., grows at an exponential rate). All in all, there is plenty of evidence that suggests that business processes are not linear, at least not all the time.

Unfortunately, there exists an infinite number of ways in which a process can deviate from linearity, and it is often impossible to know the true functional relationship. In Section 4.2, we have argued that one way of approximating the true relationship is via suitable transformation(s) of the response (Y), the predictor (X), or both. Unfortunately, we have also seen that such an approach involves a lot of guesswork and trial and error. A case in point is the price and demand data from Table 4.2. For that data, we "experimented" with three different data transformations (see also Figure 4.14) and concluded that, while the log-log transformation does not appear to be optimal, it is better than the two other alternatives (and definitely beats the linear model, in which none of the variables are transformed). But if the log-log regression model is not optimal, which one is? Unfortunately, it is impossible to know since there exist an infinite number of alternatives. To make matters worse, of all the alternatives that do exist, we may only be aware of a small subset. Ask yourself the following question: How many analytical functions do you know? Your answer may include functions such as polynomials and exponential, logarithmic, and trigonometric functions, but did it also include the *sawtooth wave function* or *Euler's totient function*? If the answer is no, then you are already missing out on some potentially important functional relationships, not because you choose to but simply because of unawareness. Thus, we can never be sure we have included every single possible functional relationship in our search for the best possible transformation. Moreover, some business relationships may not follow any *known* function at all. Thus, do you really want to spend endless hours and days looking for the "perfect" data transformation? Or, would you prefer to have available a method that can unveil the best possible relationship (or at least a very good approximation to it) *automatically* from the data? If your answer is the latter, then you should read on.

In the following section, we will discuss and illustrate *nonparametric regression*. The appeal of nonparametric regression is that it can uncover (and subsequently model) very complex functional relationships from the data in an automated fashion. The term "nonparametric" refers to the fact that this method does not make any "parametric assumptions." In fact, it does not assume any functional relationship between the response and the predictor, at least in theory. That is, unlike linear regression, which *assumes* that X and Y are related in a linear fashion, nonparametric regression abstains from any such assumption. All it "assumes" is that there is *some* relationship.[5] It will then *approximate* that relationship to a very high degree – in fact, one appeal of the method is that the degree of the approximation can be controlled by the investigator; that is, we can decide whether we want a very close approximation or whether a rather crude representation is good enough.

As pointed out in the introduction to this section, no lunch is free. While nonparametric regression can be extremely powerful at unearthing the true underlying relationship, it has one main disadvantage: insight and interpretability. In fact, because it does not make any assumptions about the relationship between the response and the predictor, the lessons that can be learned from its application are also limited. To make things more concrete, one of the main appeals of *linear regression* is that linear relationships are easily understood and conveniently interpreted. For instance, everyone can relate to a statement such as "For each increase in salary by $1,000, a customer spends $200 more at my store"; see also Section 4.3. Similarly, a log-log regression model can result in a very intuitive interpretation such as "If we increase price by 1%, then demand decreases by 2%"; see also Section 4.2.2. In fact, some data transformations (especially logarithmic ones) lend themselves to very intuitive and appealing interpretations (e.g., in terms of price elasticities, which "make sense" to managers). Unfortunately, nonparametric regression models typically do not allow such insightful takeaways, and the reason is exactly the *lack* of any assumption about the functional form. This is not to say that nonparametric

---

[5]If there was no relationship between X and Y, a model would not make any sense.

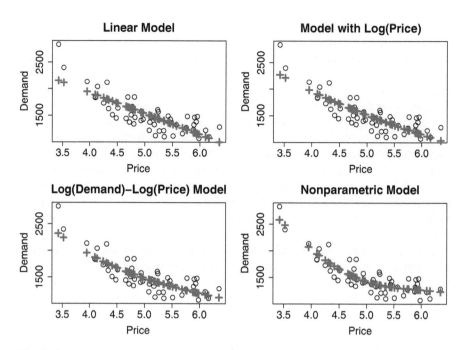

Fig. 6.13 Four different regression models. The circles correspond to the actual data; the crosses show the fits of different regression models. The top left panel shows the fits of a linear regression model; the top right panel shows a model with price log-transformed (but demand unchanged); the bottom left panel shows a log-log model (that is, both price and demand log-transformed); and the graph at the bottom right shows the fit of a nonparametric regression model.

regression methods do not allow any insight at all; we may still learn, for example, that "price has a negative relationship with demand" and that "the rate at which increasing prices reduce demand is diminishing." But typically we can no longer find out exactly *how much* this rate is diminishing.

While nonparametric regression models are limited in their ability to provide insight, they are often very powerful at providing accurate *predictions*. We have discussed in Section 6.1 that getting insight into past relationships and predicting the future may sometimes be quite contrary objectives. Since nonparametric methods can capture the nature of nonlinear relationships very well, they can potentially be very accurate at predicting even very complex business processes. And such predictive power often outweighs its limitations with respect to intuition and insight. For instance, a product manager may be much more interested in an accurate *prediction* of how an item's demand reacts to changes in price than *understanding* exactly the precise reason for this reaction.

Back to the Price and Demand Data: To make our discussion more concrete, consider again the price and demand data from Table 4.2. Figure 6.13 shows a scatterplot of that data (indicated by the circles in the graph) together with the fits

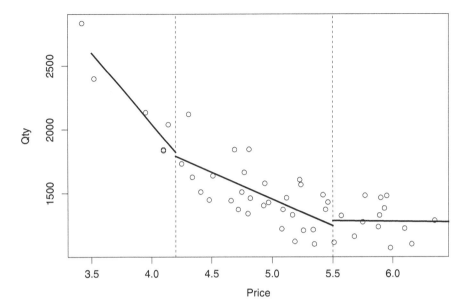

Fig. 6.14 Illustration of piecewise regression for the price and demand data. The dashed vertical lines mark the boundaries for different data segments; the thick solid lines show the regression models for each data segment.

of different regression models (indicated by the crosses). In particular, it shows the fit of a linear model (top left), a model with price log-transformed (top right), a log-log model (bottom left), and a nonparametric regression model (bottom right). Visual inspection reveals that the nonparametric model results in the best data fit. In fact, the nonparametric approach best captures the rapid "flattening out" of the data pattern as price increases. In other words, while the log-log model also captures the slow-down in demand decrease as price increases, it does not quite capture the *speed* at which it decreases. In fact, that speed is so fast that for prices higher than, say, $5.50, demand is barely reduced any further (i.e., it almost flattens out). Such a rapid change is hard to capture by any functional relationship; in contrast, the nonparametric approach (which does not rely on any functional assumptions) captures that pattern with ease.

The Idea of Nonparametric Regression Models: The nonparametric regression model in the bottom right corner of Figure 6.13 captures the observed data pattern extremely well. But how does it accomplish such an excellent data fit? The idea is actually relatively simple: rather than fitting a single function to the *entire data*, wouldn't it be possible to first *split up* the data into convenient subsegments and then fit different functions to each segment separately? The answer is "yes," and the corresponding idea is often referred to as *piecewise regression modeling*.

Consider Figure 6.14 as an illustration. In that figure, we split up the data into three segments, indicated by the vertical, dashed lines. In particular, we split the

```
Call:
lm(formula = Qty ~ Price, data = data1)

Residuals:
     26        27        45
-178.95    33.76   145.19

Coefficients:
              Estimate Std. Error  t value  Pr(>|t|)
(Intercept)     6478.4      2127.1    3.046     0.202
Price          -1108.6       584.8   -1.896     0.309

Residual standard error: 232.9 on 1 degrees of freedom
Multiple R-squared: 0.7823,      Adjusted R-squared: 0.5646
F-statistic: 3.594 on 1 and 1 DF,  p-value: 0.309
```

Fig. 6.15 Regression estimates for the first data segment (i.e., for all data with prices lower than $4.20).

data into a first segment that includes only prices between $3 and $4.20, a second segment containing all records with prices between $4.20 and $5.50, and a third segment with prices at $5.50 and above. After segmenting the data in this fashion, we now fit a linear regression model to each segment. That is, we are estimating three separate models, one for each data segment. Since the data pattern in each segment is very different, we would expect the resulting regression models to be very different from one another. In particular, we would expect the slope in the first segment to be much steeper than the one in the third segment. Indeed, Figures 6.15–6.17 show the corresponding regression estimates. We can see that the slope is as steep as −1,108.6 in segment one (Figure 6.15) but gradually reduces to −10.75 for the third data-segment (Figure 6.17).

Next, we "piece" the three individual models back together and overlay them on the original (entire) data set. The result is given by the three solid lines in Figure 6.14. We can see that, taken together, these three individual regression lines capture the overall trend in the data very well. Thus, running individual regression models on smaller "pieces" of the entire data, we can capture even very complicated patterns – this idea is generally referred to as "piecewise regression." However, rather than estimating three separate models, piecewise regression estimates one single model but does so in a way that accommodates different patterns in different data segments. The reason that we prefer running a single model (rather than three individual ones) is the loss of power typically incurred by splitting the data into smaller subpieces.

While the piecewise regressions in Figure 6.14 capture the overall trend very well, there are still several shortcomings. First, the three regression lines are not connected. In fact, there are rather large "gaps" at the boundaries of our segments (at $4.20 and $5.50, respectively). Moreover, even if the gaps disappeared, the lines still would not connect in a smooth fashion – a smooth connection between individual line components is essential for subsequent analytical operations such as

```
Call:
lm(formula = Qty ~ Price, data = data2)

Residuals:
   Min      1Q  Median      3Q     Max
-253.90 -137.51  -40.28  111.75  374.61

Coefficients:
             Estimate Std. Error t value Pr(>|t|)
(Intercept)   3554.0     365.7    9.719 6.30e-11 ***
Price         -419.9      75.2   -5.583 4.04e-06 ***
---
Signif. codes:  0 '***' 0.001 '**' 0.01 '*' 0.05 '.' 0.1 ' ' 1

Residual standard error: 176.6 on 31 degrees of freedom
Multiple R-squared: 0.5014,     Adjusted R-squared: 0.4853
F-statistic: 31.17 on 1 and 31 DF,  p-value: 4.036e-06
```

Fig. 6.16 Regression estimates for the second data segment (i.e., for all data with prices between $4.20 and $5.50).

```
Call:
lm(formula = Qty ~ Price, data = data3)

Residuals:
    Min       1Q   Median       3Q      Max
-208.002 -105.348    0.751   88.353  200.741

Coefficients:
             Estimate Std. Error t value Pr(>|t|)
(Intercept)  1343.30    1046.13    1.284   0.223
Price         -10.75     177.58   -0.061   0.953

Residual standard error: 145 on 12 degrees of freedom
Multiple R-squared: 0.0003054,  Adjusted R-squared: -0.083
F-statistic: 0.003666 on 1 and 12 DF,  p-value: 0.9527
```

Fig. 6.17 Regression estimates for the third data segment (i.e., for all data with prices higher than $5.50).

taking derivatives. And finally, while fitting three linear lines to the data segments appears like a good start, nothing prevents us from fitting more flexible functional relationships such as quadratic or cubic functions. All three of these shortcomings are addressed in the so-called *smoothing spline*. A smoothing spline consists of the following components:

- It is a *piecewise polynomial*. As such, it allows for the same flexibility as in Figure 6.14; however, it is not limited only to linear functions but accommodates polynomials of any order (which addresses the third shortcoming above).

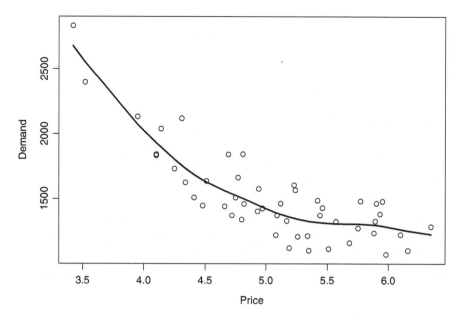

Fig. 6.18 Smoothing spline for the price and demand data.

- It assures that pieces are connected in a *smooth* and *continuous* fashion, which addresses shortcomings 1 and 2.
- In addition, it contains a *penalty term*, which assures that the resulting function is not too variable (or "wiggly").

A smoothing spline for the price and demand data can be found in Figure 6.18. We can see that it captures the observed pattern in the data in a very accurate fashion.

Interpreting a Nonparametric Regression Model: Nonparametric regression models put the ideas of smoothing splines into a modeling framework. In fact, the nonparametric regression model for the price and demand data could formally be written as

$$\text{Demand} = a + s(\text{Price}) \tag{6.13}$$

where the notation $s(\text{Price})$ denotes a *smooth* function of price. In particular, note that we no longer write $(a + b \times \text{Price})$ in equation (6.13) since we no longer require a linear relationship between price and demand. On the contrary, all we require is that there be *some* relationship between these two variables, and we request that this relationship be expressed in a smooth fashion – á la a smoothing spline as in Figure 6.18.

Figure 6.19 shows the regression estimate for the nonparametric regression model in equation (6.13). We note that it is no longer expressed by a single number such as the coefficient $-1{,}108.6$ in Figure 6.15 but by a continuous line instead. In fact, this line can be interpreted as a *range* of different coefficients, a different one

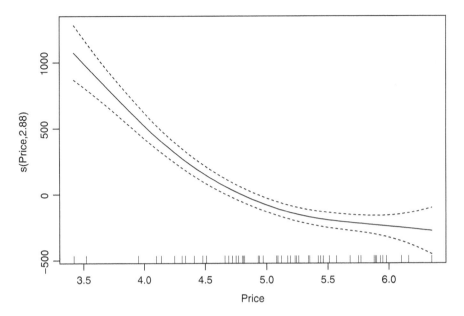

Fig. 6.19 Regression estimate for the nonparametric regression model.

for each different value of price. For instance, the value corresponding to price = $4.00 is approximately 500. This implies that if we set a price of $4, we could expect a demand of

$$\text{Demand}_{Price=\$4} = 1{,}508.64 + 500 = \$2{,}008.64 \tag{6.14}$$

since the model also estimated the intercept a to equal 1,508.64.

Figure 6.19 illustrates one of the shortcomings of nonparametric regression discussed earlier: since the relationship between price and demand is presented in the form of a graph (rather than a single number), the result does not lend itself easily to very deep interpretations. To be sure, we can still deduce from Figure 6.19 that there is a *negative relationship* between price and demand and that the *strength of the relationship* slowly decreases (i.e., the curve in Figure 6.19 slowly flattens out). However, it falls short of providing us insight into the precise nature of that relationship, as we can no longer quantify *how much* the strength of this relationship declines. In that sense, the model in equation (6.13) (and the corresponding model estimate in Figure 6.19) have limited interpretability.

Predictive Performance of Nonparametric Regression: While the nonparametric regression model may not be as easy and convenient to interpret as a linear regression model, it has the ability to provide superior predictive performance. Table 6.10 shows the performance of the model in equation (6.13) on a test set. Similar to

Table 6.10 RMSE and MAE for the nonparametric regression model compared with the three parametric models from Figure 6.13. "Linear" refers to a linear regression model with neither price nor demand transformed; "Log(Price)" refers to the model with only price log-transformed (but demand unchanged); and "Log(Demand) and Log(Price)" refers to a log-log model where both price and demand are log-transformed.

Model	RMSE	MAE
Nonparametric	202.1596	153.4174
Linear	278.3518	175.3153
Log(Price)	252.3319	163.8205
Log(Demand) and Log(Price)	253.9469	171.0894

the ideas outlined in Section 6.1, we again split the data into a training set and a test set. We again choose to reserve 70% of the data for the training set, which leaves 30% for the test set. As before, allocate data in random fashion to each of the two sets. Table 6.10 shows the values of RMSE and MAE for the nonparametric model compared with the three linear models from Figure 6.13: one more that uses price and demand in their original form ("Linear"), another model that log-transforms price but leaves demand unchanged ("Log(Price)"), and a third model in which both price and demand are log-transformed ("Log(Demand) and Log(Price)").

We can see that the nonparametric model results in the best predictive performance. This is not too surprising since we have already argued that this model is best at capturing the complex pattern in the data. Neither the linear model nor its log-transformed variants can capture the pattern adequately and hence cannot predict future demand as accurately. The managerial implication is that while the nonparametric model does not provide as much deep insight into the economic relationships between price and demand, it is much more accurate at anticipating changes in demand as a result of changes in pricing strategies. Thus, if the objective is to maximize demand (say, given certain cost restrictions), then the nonparametric model could result in much smarter pricing strategies and ultimately lead to higher revenues for the firm.

Lessons Learned:

- Not all business processes can be captured well using linear models. While transformations of the data may render more realistic relationships in light of known laws such as "diminishing returns," they may not result in the best possible approximation to the observed data pattern.
- Nonparametric regression models promise to capture even complex relationships without making any assumptions about the functional form. The main idea of nonparametric methods is to approximate the observed pattern in the data via "smooth pieces."

> • Nonparametric regression models have both advantages and disadvantages. While they can capture observed trends and patterns very well, they usually do not generate rich economic insight into the cause of these patterns. On the other hand, because of their ability to recover complex data patterns, they often generate very accurate forecasts and predictions.

6.3   Data Case: Fine-Tuning Stock Price Prediction Models

We now apply the lessons learned from this chapter to fine-tune the financial indicator model from Section 5.2. In particular, we will investigate *how much better* we can predict a company's stock price using regression trees or nonparametric regression models introduced in Section 6.2. Our goal is purely *predictive*; that is, we will focus exclusively on how well we can anticipate a company's stock price (using the concept of a training set and a test set) and ignore its fit to observed (i.e., past) data (see also Section 6.1). The rationale is that as a market analyst (or investor) we would be primarily interested in the *future* performance of our investment and base our trading decisions on our anticipation of future changes in stock price.

We pointed out in Section 5.2 that modeling the financial indicator data in Table 5.3 is complex since it consists of a total of 25 different variables. Thus – so we have argued – variable selection via stepwise regression could be beneficial in selecting some of the more important variables. However, we have also seen in Figure 5.13 that many of the variables are highly skewed and, as a result, show only rather weak correlation with a company's stock price. As a consequence, we have applied a logarithmic transformation to the data that renders variables with less skew and stronger correlations (see also Figure 5.14). In fact, stepwise regression applied to the log-transformed data results in a model with a much better fit (Figure 5.16) compared with its application to the untransformed data (Figure 5.12). But does this better data fit also translate into more accurate predictions? And is the model in Figure 5.16 the best possible model to anticipate a company's stock price?

In order to answer these questions, we compare the performance of stepwise regression with that of a regression tree and a nonparametric regression model. In fact, we compare the performance on both the original (i.e., untransformed) data and the log-transformed data. The reason is that alternate model specifications do not necessarily replace data transformations. While a nonparametric regression model can capture nonlinear patterns in the data automatically, it may capture patterns even better *after* a data transformation. Moreover, regression trees are capable of detecting complex interactions but cannot correct nonlinearities; thus, a regression tree applied to transformed data may perform better than one applied to the original data. In other words, while some of the more advanced methods discussed in Section 6.2 may alleviate our worries about nonlinear patterns in the data, it is good practice to apply them *in conjunction* with data transformations and other activities to make our data more fit for modeling.[6] Or, put differently one more time, when modeling complex sets of data, we should consider applying all of the tools at our disposal rather than only limiting our attention to one or two methods.

We compare the performances of a total of eight different models: four models are estimated on the original (i.e., untransformed) data, and another four models are estimated on the log-transformed data. For each set of models, we use the following specifications:

- *Kitchen Sink*: We start with the "kitchen sink" model in Figure 5.9. That is, our benchmark model contains all 24 predictor variables from Table 5.3. We have already argued earlier that this model provides a rather poor fit to the data, so we would not expect too much from it. However, since we have not yet investigated its predictive capabilities, we start our investigations with this comprehensive model. We investigate its performance applied to both the original (untransformed) data and the log-transformed data. When applying this model to the log-transformed data, all variables (including the target variable "stock price") are subjected to a logarithmic transformation.

- *Stepwise Regression*: The second model we investigate is the result of a stepwise regression procedure applied to the entire set of variables. We again apply stepwise regression both to the original (untransformed) data and the log-transformed data. We have already seen the result in Figure 5.12 (for the original data), and in Figure 5.16 (for the log-transformed data) and concluded that the logarithmic transformation results in a much better data fit. But we do not yet know whether the better fit to the observed data also implies higher predictive accuracy.

- *Regression Tree*: We apply the regression tree to both the original data and the log-transformed data. In fact, we apply the tree to all 24 predictor variables from Table 5.3. The reason is that regression trees, besides their ability to unveil complex interactions, also serve as an alternative vehicle for variable selection. In fact, a predictor that does not show up in a tree is less likely to be important for prediction. Thus, trees are often used as a complementary tool to stepwise regression procedures.

- *Nonparametric Regression*: Nonparametric regression methods can reduce the effect of nonlinear relationships but – unlike regression trees – they do not perform any sort of variable selection. In fact, nonparametric regression models – like standard (linear) regression models – operate on the variables that we input, so it is our responsibility to "feed" them the right variables. To that end, we apply nonparametric regression to the variables selected by stepwise regression. In fact, we apply the method to both the output of stepwise regression based on the original data (Figure 5.12) and the log-transformed data (Figure 5.16). We refer to the resulting model as *stepwise and nonparametric regression*.

---

[6]Some of these additional activities may include the close investigation of outliers or extreme events and their potential removal from the data.

Table 6.11 Predictive performance of regression trees and nonparametric regression for the financial indicator data from Table 5.3. We compare the methods the "kitchen sink" linear regression model as well as the result of stepwise regression variable selection. We compare the methods both on the original data (i.e., without applying any transformation to the variables) and the log-transformed data; for the log-transformed data, all variables are subjected to a logarithmic transformation. We measure the predictive performance on a test set. That is, we estimate all models on the same training set; we then compare their predictive accuracy on a test set that is also identical across all models. We again measure predictive accuracy in terms of root mean squared error (RMSE) and mean absolute error (MAE).

Log-Transformation	Model	RMSE	MAE
No	Kitchen Sink	1531.86	137.24
No	Regression Tree	31.82	18.20
No	Stepwise Regression	19.13	14.74
No	Stepwise & Nonparametric Regression	18.97	14.64
Yes	Kitchen Sink	118.92	21.60
Yes	Regression Tree	25.22	16.92
Yes	Stepwise Regression	70.44	17.56
Yes	Stepwise & Nonparametric Regression	17.36	13.27

The result is shown in Table 6.11. The first column indicates whether or not the data has been log-transformed; the first four models are estimated on the original (i.e., untransformed) data, while for the last four models the data has been log-transformed. The second columns indicates the type of the model as described above. The third and fourth columns show the predictive accuracy of each model measured on a test set. For that test set, we randomly partition the data into 70% of the records for training purposes and use the remaining 30% for testing their predictive accuracy.

We can make the following observations:

- *The Loser*: The "kitchen sink" model fares extremely poorly. On the original data, its RMSE is two orders of magnitude higher than all the other models. This suggests that the data is extremely skewed (since RMSE measures the *squared error*, it is affected more by outliers than MAE) and that it contains too much useless information. In fact, we have already seen that many of the 25 variables are correlated with one another. Thus, including all of them in a single model results in a feature that is often referred to as "fitting noise": the *signal* in the data is of much smaller dimension, so, by including all possible variables, the model essentially mistakes some of the *noise* for a signal and hence predicts poorly. Applying the kitchen sink model to the log-transformed data results in a slightly better performance. The reason is that many of the data patterns become more linear after a logarithmic transformation; see also Figure 5.14. But overall its performance is still very poor compared with the remaining models because it still contains too many useless predictors and overfits the data.

- *Improvements*: Both stepwise regression and the regression tree improve tremendously over the kitchen sink model. It is interesting that while stepwise regression results in a better performance on the original data, the regression tree has a smaller prediction error for the log-transformed data. This shows that both stepwise regression and regression trees are capable of performing variable selection and both should be consulted when modeling large and complex sets of data.
- *The Winner*: The winner is the nonparametric regression model applied to the output of stepwise regression. This model results in the highest predictive accuracy, both on the original data and on the log-transformed data. In fact, the most accurate forecasts of a company's stock price are accomplished when using the nonparametric model on the log-transformed data. This shows that while nonparametric methods are capable of capturing nonlinearities in the data, their performance can be improved by first rendering the data "more linear" (using a data transformation in this case). It also shows that statistical methods are best used in combination: the overall winner of this modeling exercise consists of three different modeling components:

1. a transformation of the original data (logarithmic in this case),
2. variable selection via stepwise regression, and
3. capturing the remaining nonlinearities in the data via a nonparametric model.

Data Segmentation: A final look at the winning model is in order. Figure 6.20 shows the size of the error for the nonparametric regression model based on stepwise regression of the log-transformed data (i.e., the last model in Table 6.11) plotted against the actual stock price. We can see that while the model predicts stocks with lower prices (say between $0 and $40) rather evenly, it systematically underpredicts stocks with higher values and errs especially highly for the stocks with the highest prices. This suggests that our final model may still need additional adjustments. Such adjustments could include a *segmentation strategy* (where investments are first classified as, say, "high"-vs. "low"-value stocks, and subsequently separate models are estimated for each segment separately). In other words, data modeling is like a never-ending story where improvements can be found every time we re-inspect the data in a different way.

Lessons Learned:

- The main lesson learned in this section is that statistical methods should never be applied in a "silo-style fashion." In fact, when modeling large and complex sets of data, one should bring *all* of the tools and methods to the table that are available. This may include data transformations *and* variable selection *and* models for complex interactions and nonlinearities. The more tools and methods that one investigates, the higher the chances of finding a better model. In the context of our example, the *combination* of a logarithmic transformation *and* stepwise regression *and* nonparametric

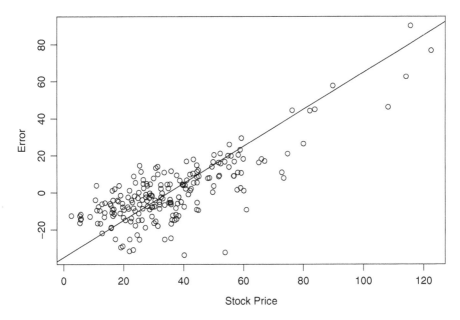

Fig. 6.20 Error of the winning model relative to the actual stock price. The graph shows the size of the error for the nonparametric regression model based on stepwise regression of the log-transformed data (i.e., the last model in Table 6.11) plotted against the actual stock price.

modeling results in the best model. But we have also argued that the best model that we found may not be the *universally* best model. Models can always be improved. In fact, one should only stop investigating further model improvements when time and resources demand a solution *now*. In most situations, one will be able to further improve the current solution by investigating additional ideas or methods. One such method could be a *segmentation approach* that would allow us to treat subsegments of the data in a different fashion. In other words, when modeling complex data, one is never truly *done*. While one may have found a solution that is better than all other current alternatives, there is always opportunity for further improvement. In addition, the world changes while we are investigating different modeling alternatives. Thus, good models should be able to account for such changes and *adaptively* react to new environments.

Chapter 7
Appendix: Introduction to the Statistical Software R

The analyses in this book were conducted using the statistical software R. While similar analyses could have been assembled using different software solutions, we want to provide a quick introduction to R. R has two main advantages compared with many of its competitors:

- R is free. It is based on an open source project and free of charge.
- R grows on a daily basis. Since R is an open source project, researchers contribute to it every day. This means that R provides the most up-to-date and most complete solution possible.

In the following, we provide a quick start to R. By no means is this chapter meant to be exhaustive in covering all aspects of R. Rather, the goal is to provide the basic steps necessary to quickly get up and running with R.

In order to mine data with R, we only need a few basic steps. First, we need to download and install the R software. After installing R, we need to understand how to start it, how to load data into it, how to execute statistical functions to analyze our data, and how to export the results of our analyses. We will also discuss some basic R data manipulations as it is often necessary, especially for advanced analytics, to first manipulate the data before extracting intelligence from it. Also, one of the main advantages of R is its unparalleled amount of "libraries" (a library is an add-on package that adds extra functionality to the software). There are special libraries for analyzing geographical data, and other libraries for creating interactive graphs. We will make extensive use of libraries in this book. And finally, there exist "graphical user interfaces" (GUIs) that further facilitate the use of R. GUIs basically allow a "point-and-click" interaction with R and are especially useful the novice user. We will discuss GUIs in the final section of this chapter.

7.1 How and Where Do I Get R?

R is available for free and can be downloaded from the link http://cran.r-project.
org/. This site hosts the basic software and add-on packages, as well as a ton of
auxiliary material. A quick way to find this link is to type "CRAN" into Google.

Once you arrive at the CRAN homepage, locate the section for "Download and
Install R" and then click on the link corresponding to your operating system (Linux,
Mac, or Windows). In the following, I will assume that you are using a Windows
operating system, but the procedure is very similar for the two other alternatives.

After you click on "Windows," you will find two further links, "base" and
"contrib" – you want to select the link for "base." The next page will feature a link
to "Download R X.X.X," where "X.X.X" denotes the most recent version of R; for
instance, at the time of writing this book, the most recent version was 2.9.1, so the
link read "Download R 2.9.1." Click on that link and follow all further instructions
of the download and installation process.

Notice that there have been some issues with installing R under Windows Vista.
(In fact, Windows Vista has had issues with many different software packages, not
only R.) Basically, file permissions are handled differently under Windows Vista and
need to be adjusted when installing R. If you are a Vista user, then please carefully
read the "Frequently Asked Questions" on the R download page.

After installation of the software is complete, you will find an "R" icon on your
desktop – starting R is as easy as double-clicking on that icon.

7.2 How Do I Get Started with R?

We are now in a position to use R for the very first time. Locate the R icon on
your desktop and double-click it. You will see a window appear (the "R Console")
similar to the one in Figure 7.1; this console is the main interface between you and
the software.

In order to use R, you need to enter text at the prompt; the prompt is the red arrow
marked by ">". To interact with the software, you enter text at the prompt and then
hit "Enter." For instance, if you type

```
5
```

and then hit "Enter," you will see

```
[1] 5
```

which is R's way of confirming that you just entered the number 5. A more
meaningful interaction with R would be of the form

```
5 + 3
```

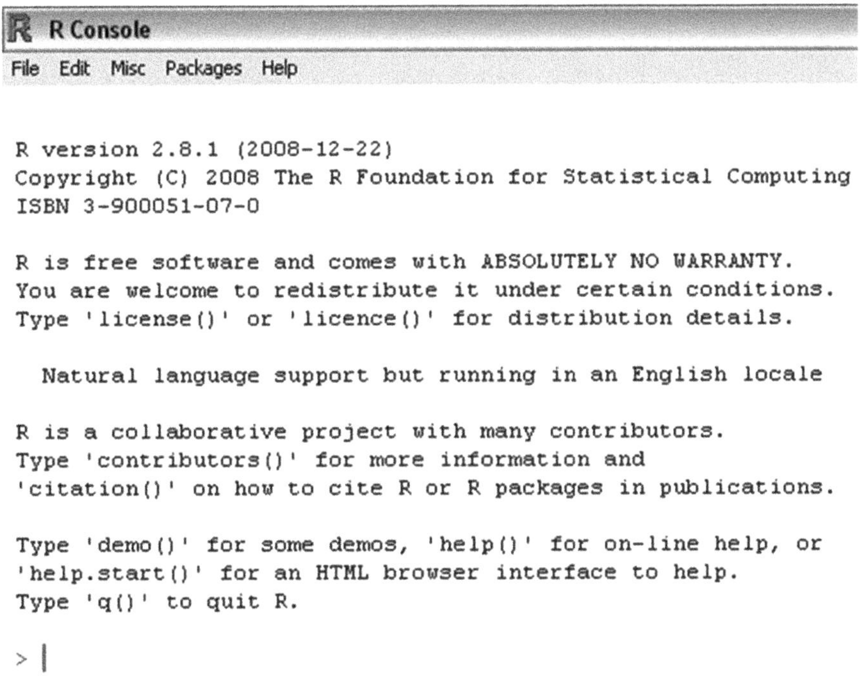

```
R  R Console
File  Edit  Misc  Packages  Help

R version 2.8.1 (2008-12-22)
Copyright (C) 2008 The R Foundation for Statistical Computing
ISBN 3-900051-07-0

R is free software and comes with ABSOLUTELY NO WARRANTY.
You are welcome to redistribute it under certain conditions.
Type 'license()' or 'licence()' for distribution details.

  Natural language support but running in an English locale

R is a collaborative project with many contributors.
Type 'contributors()' for more information and
'citation()' on how to cite R or R packages in publications.

Type 'demo()' for some demos, 'help()' for on-line help, or
'help.start()' for an HTML browser interface to help.
Type 'q()' to quit R.

> |
```

Fig. 7.1 R's main window after startup; the window is also called the R Console; the prompt is given by the red arrow (>) at the bottom of the figure.

followed by "Enter," which returns

    [1] 8

(see also Figure 7.2). In other words, R tells you that the result of adding the two numbers $5 + 3$ equals 8 – which is what we expected. This also shows that R, in its most basic form, can be used as a calculator! Not convinced yet? Then try to multiply the two numbers 4 and 5; to do that, you type

    4 * 5

followed by "Enter," which returns

    [1] 20

R is that easy to use! In the following, we will omit the explicit instruction to hit "Enter" every single time we type an R command; rather, every time we discuss an R command, we assume that it is followed by an execution of "Enter."

```
R  R Console

File  Edit  Misc  Packages  Help


R version 2.8.1 (2008-12-22)
Copyright (C) 2008 The R Foundation for Statistical Computing
ISBN 3-900051-07-0

R is free software and comes with ABSOLUTELY NO WARRANTY.
You are welcome to redistribute it under certain conditions.
Type 'license()' or 'licence()' for distribution details.

   Natural language support but running in an English locale

R is a collaborative project with many contributors.
Type 'contributors()' for more information and
'citation()' on how to cite R or R packages in publications.

Type 'demo()' for some demos, 'help()' for on-line help, or
'help.start()' for an HTML browser interface to help.
Type 'q()' to quit R.
```

```
> 5+3
[1] 8
>
```

Fig. 7.2 A first interaction with R. To add the numbers 5 and 3, type "5+3" at the prompt and then hit "Enter"; the result $(5 + 3 = 8)$ is displayed underneath.

7.3   Basic R Manipulations

We have seen in the previous section that R can be used as a calculator. In fact, there are many standard arithmetic operations that we can readily perform in R. Besides adding or multiplying two numbers, we can also subtract or divide them. For instance, subtracting 5 from 10 is done by typing

```
10 - 5
```

And we can divide 20 by 5 by typing

```
20 / 4
```

R also knows powers or logarithmic functions. For instance, if we want to compute the square root of 9, we type

```
sqrt(9)
```

And computing the (natural) logarithm of 10 is done by typing

```
log(10)
```

But its ability as a calculator is not the main reason for using R. One important feature of R is its ability to assign data values to variables. For instance, assume that the unit cost for a product equals $10. Then we can tell R to remember that number by typing

```
cost <- 10
```

Notice that the left arrow "<-" assigns the number 10 to the variable "cost"; we could have also used a different name for this variable, but "cost" seemed like a natural choice. Assume further that the unit price for the product above equals $20. We again tell R to remember that number by typing

```
price <- 20
```

Now, assume that we sold 100 units of that product. Then we can compute the net income as

```
net.income <- 100 * (price - cost)
```

Now, you ask, "What is the final net income figure?" R knows it and you can get R's answer by typing

```
net.income
```

The result will be shown as

```
[1] 1000
```

In other words, net income equals $1,000. What did we learn from the example above? We learned that we can use variables to tell R to save data values (such as cost or price), that we can perform calculations on these variables (such as the net income calculation, which is a function of price and cost), and that if we assign another variable name to the net income calculation, then we have to actively ask R for its value (i.e., type the variable name "net.income") in order to see the results.

Variables are a powerful concept in R. In fact, R refers to these variables as "objects" because you can use them to save and remember all kinds of different data and information. Throughout this book, we will use variables to perform operations on single data values or even entire datasets. In the next section, we describe how to load datasets into R.

7.4   Loading Data, Executing Functions, and Exporting Results

This book deals with deriving analytics from data. In that sense, we'll be mostly concerned with situations where a set of data is readily available and we want to analyze that data using R. To that end, we first have to get that data into R. Loading

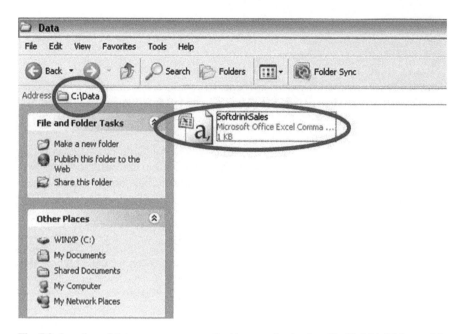

Fig. 7.3 Location of data on our computer: In this example, the data file "SoftdrinkSales.csv" is located on our C drive in a folder called "Data"; hence the path is C:\\Data.

data into R can be done in many different ways, and we will only describe a few of them here. We will assume throughout that your data arrives in a spreadsheet format (e.g., as an Excel spreadsheet or as a comma-separated file). While one can also upload differently formatted data files into R, we will not discuss those approaches here.

Consider the data in the file SoftdrinkSales.csv (see also Figure 7.3). Notice that this data has been formatted as a comma-separated file (hence the file extension .csv). But notice also that we can easily open the data into, For example, Microsoft Excel by double-clicking it. If we open the file, we see that there are two columns, SALES and ADVT (where "ADVT" stands for "Advertising"). Our goal is first to upload the data into R and subsequently analyze it.

Uploading data into R is a two-step procedure: we first have to tell R where the data is located (i.e., we have to specify the "working directory") and then have to read the data file from that directory.

Let's assume that you have saved the file SoftdrinkSales.csv on your C drive ("C:") inside a folder called "Data" as in Figure 7.3. Then, under Windows Explorer, the location of your file would be denoted as "C:\Data". Thus, in the first step, we have to tell R that this is the location of your working directory. This is done via the command setwd(). In our case, we type

```
setwd(''C:\\Data'')
```

Notice the double-backslash ("\\") and also that both the quotation marks are closing quotes (" ") inside the parentheses – these details are important. Omission or modification of any of these details will lead to an error message. For instance, if we forget to type the second quotation mark

```
setwd(''C:\\Data)
```

then R will complain and return

```
> setwd(''C:\\Data)
+
```

where the "+" indicates that R is expecting further input. In other words, R is telling you that the previous command is incomplete and you'd better start all over again! You can start all over again by hitting the escape key ("Esc") on your keyboard and then retype the entire command.

After setting our working directory to "C:\\Data", we can now proceed to step two. In that step, we read our data from the file SoftdrinkSales.csv. This is done via the command read.csv since our file is in comma-separated format. We type

```
read.csv(''SoftdrinkSales.csv'')
```

We can see that all the data from the file SoftdrinkSales.csv now appears in the R Console window (see also Figure 7.4). This is great, but as our goal is to analyze the data rather than merely look at it, this is not too useful yet. Hence we modify our previous step and type

```
data <- read.csv(''SoftdrinkSales.csv'')
```

(see also bottom the of Figure 7.4). Now we have uploaded the file and saved it as an object that we ominously called "data," and are now ready to extract knowledge from that data.

Before jumping into analyses that are too complex, it is good practice to verify that the data that we just uploaded into R is what we had expected and matches the data in the original file SoftdrinkSales.csv. To that end, we should at least check the data's variable names and dimensions. We can check the data's names by typing

```
names(data)
```

This returns

```
[1] ''SALES'' ''ADVT''
```

which matches our expectations. We also may want to check the dimensions of our data; by dimensions we mean the number of rows and columns. Note that the original file SoftdrinkSales.csv has 25 rows (excluding the first row for the names) and 2 columns. We can check whether the uploaded data matches those dimensions by typing

```
dim(data)
```

```
R   R Console
File   Edit   Misc   Packages   Help

>  setwd("C:\\Data")
>  read.csv("SoftdrinkSales.csv")
     SALES ADVT
1    145.1  9.5
2    128.3 10.1
3    121.3  9.4
4    134.4 11.6
5    106.5 10.3
6    111.5  9.5
7    132.7 11.2
8    126.9  9.0
9    151.0 11.0
10   123.3  8.4
11   154.6 11.2
12   108.0  8.8
13   159.3 11.9
14   136.3  9.8
15   111.4 11.2
16   133.6  9.6
17   137.0  9.3
18   112.9 10.0
19   122.1  8.4
20   140.5 10.5
21   141.5 11.8
22    88.5  9.0
23   127.7 10.2
24   130.7 11.8
25   122.3 10.4
>  data <- read.csv("SoftdrinkSales.csv")
>  |
```

Fig. 7.4   Data from SoftdrinkSales.csv.

This returns

```
[1]  25 2
```

which we interpret as 25 rows and 2 columns, hence our uploaded data is an exact match. We can now move on to analyzing the data.

While we will discuss more detailed analyses in the subsequent chapters, we want to give a quick taste of the general principles here. Analyzing data in R is typically done by executing a variety of functions. For instance, there are functions that compute the average for a set of numbers, or their standard deviation. More complex functions compute a regression model or perform a classification analysis. While the specific functions will vary from analysis to analysis, the principle is always the same: any function will need input in the form of a set of data (or a subset of the data) followed by optional parameters. For instance, if we want to compute the mean values for both sales and advertising, we type

```
mean(data)
```

This results in

```
SALES ADVT
128.296 10.156
```

On the other hand, if we only wanted the mean values for sales (ignoring advertising), we would type

```
mean(data$SALES)
```

Note that `data$SALES` tells R to use only the column of data that pertains to sales and ignore all other data. We can apply the same principle and tell R to plot sales against advertising by typing

```
plot(data$ADVT, data$SALES)
```

which produces a scatterplot of sales and advertising. Note that we again specifically instructed R to use the sales portion and the advertising portion of the data separately.

Finally, after using R to analyze your data, it is often useful to export the results. Many people like to export their analyses into a spreadsheet so they can use them in subsequent reporting. Exporting results into spreadsheets is possible via the command `write.csv`. Let's consider the following example.

We continue to analyze the soft drink sales data above. We can obtain summary statistics for the data using the command `summary`. For instance, typing

```
summary(data)
```

returns the minimum and maximum, mean and median, and the first and third quartiles for both sales and advertising. Now, let's export these summary statistics into a new spreadsheet. We type

```
write.csv(summary(data), ''export.csv'')
```

Notice that this creates a new file, `export.csv`. Locate this file (you should find it in the same folder as the original sales data; i.e., in `C:\Data`) and open it. You will find the summary statistics inside.

We close this section with a final comment. So far, we have only discussed uploading commma-separated files into R. While it is also possible to upload Excel files into R, the problem with Excel is that many spreadsheets contain hidden formats or formulas that are not part of the actual data. Therefore, the author of this book prefers to first save an Excel file as a comma-separated file and then upload that comma-separated file into R. While this may seem tedious, it often prevents "unpleasant surprises" that can linger in Excel documents.

You can save any Excel worksheet as a comma-separated file in the following way. First, locate the "Save As" button and click on it. Then, when asked "Save as type," select "CSV(Comma delimited)" and hit "Save."

One more caveat: American versions of Excel actually use commas to separate entries in comma-separated files; however, European versions separate entries by semicolons – admittedly very confusing but there's nothing that we can do about it!

7.5   R Libraries

We next discuss one of the single most important aspects of R: libraries. An R library is an add-on package that increases the capabilities of R. There exist almost 2,000 add-on packages for R, and this number is growing every day. There are add-on packages for performing spatial analyses, for mining written text, for exporting to HTML code, and even for analyzing sound. These add-on packages are referred to as "libraries" and have to be individually downloaded and added to the system. We will discuss this process next.

Adding a library is a two-step process. In the first step, the package has to be downloaded and installed. Once installed, the package "lives" in the R system, but it has to be activated every time we start a new R session (i.e., every time we open a new R window).

Assume that we want to install the package "Rcmdr" (read: R commander) – it will become clear in a second why we would want to install that package. As pointed out above, we first have to download and install that package. To that end, we locate the tab for "Packages" in the R window and click on "Install package(s)...". This will bring up a query asking us to select a "mirror" (see also Figure 7.5) – a server

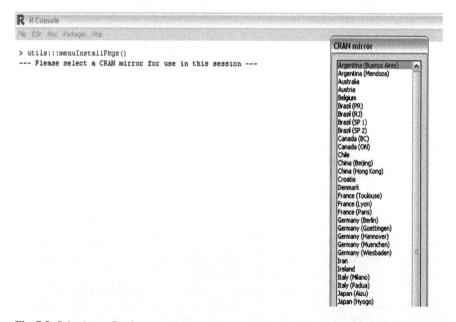

Fig. 7.5 Selecting an R mirror.

Fig. 7.6   Selecting an R package to be installed.

hosting all the R material – and we want to select the mirror that is geographically closest to us (e.g., Germany(Berlin) if we lived in Berlin or USA(NC) if we lived on the as East Coast). After selecting the mirror, another query will pop up (see also Figure 7.6). This query asks us to select a package that we would like to install. Since we want to install "Rcmdr," we scroll down until we find the corresponding entry, select it, and click "OK." You will now see an installation process and several test messages in your R window. Once the installation process is complete, the red prompt (">") will reoccur. This completes the first step.

Now, the package is installed but it is not yet active. In order to activate your package, you have two options. The first option is to go back to the "Packages" tab and select "Load package...". This will open another query (see also Figure 7.7), where you have to scroll down and select "Rcmdr." After clicking "OK," you will see another window pop up (see also Figure 7.8) – this is the R commander. (Note that when you first activate Rcmdr you may get a question asking whether you want to install additional packages – simply select "Yes.")

The second option to activate a package is via the command "library." Rather than pointing and clicking as outlined above, simply type "library(Rcmdr)" (careful: spelling is case-sensitive!) and hit "Enter" – you will see the same result as above.

As final note on this section, the steps above have installed the so-called R commander. The R commander is a graphical user interface (GUI) that makes interaction between you and the software more convenient. We will talk more about GUIs in the next section.

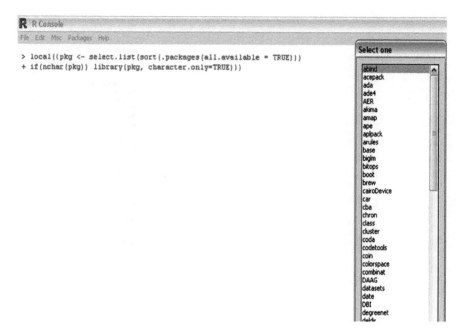

Fig. 7.7 Selecting an R package (or "library") to be activated.

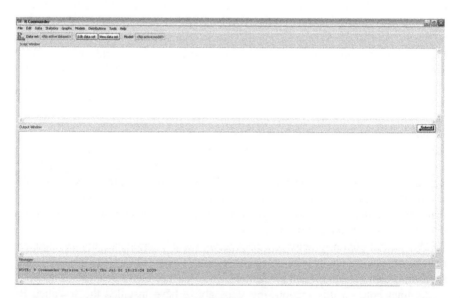

Fig. 7.8 The R Commander *Rcmdr* window.

7.6 Graphical User Interfaces

Graphical user interfaces (GUIs) are interfaces that allow people to interact with software in more ways than just by typing text. Probably the most successful and most well-known GUIs are the products of Microsoft Office. In Microsoft Excel, for instance, we can "interact" (e.g., print a page, load a file, create a graph) by simply pointing out cursor at a certain icon of the software and then clicking on that icon. This "point-and-click" interface has made Microsoft successful, and it is a reason why theirs is the most commonly used office software today. R, in its most basic form, does not possess these user-friendly capabilities; in fact, we have to type our commands into the R Console window (see, e.g., Figure 7.2). Typing our commands directly makes the initial learning experience somewhat harder; however, it also makes the software more flexible since it allows a much larger number of options for the user to customize the result. There exist several R GUIs that achieve a balance between the two: these GUIs allow the user-friendly point-and-click interaction with the software; at the same time, they also preserve much of R's flexibility. We will discuss two of the most powerful R GUIs below. These GUIs go by the name of *Rcmdr* (which stands for "R Commander") and *Rattle*. While Rcmdr is geared more toward traditional statistical analyses, Rattle internalizes the general data mining process.

7.6.1 Rcmdr

We have already discussed in Section 7.5 how to install the library *Rcmdr* so we are now in a position to use and illustrate it. If your Rcmdr window is no longer active, remember that you can reactivate it using the command "library(Rcmdr)" followed by the usual "Enter." This brings up a window just like in Figure 7.8 – your R commander is now ready for use!

Let's use it by importing the soft drink sales data from Section 7.4. To that end, locate the data tab on the top of the Rcmdr window and click on it. Several options appear (see also screen 1 in Figure 7.9); most of the time you will want to *import* an existing set of data (such as the file SoftdrinkSales.csv), so let's hover our cursor over the third option ("Import data..."), which will bring up another five options (see again screen 1 in Figure 7.9). Here, you have the option to import a text file, files from other software packages such as SPSS or Minitab, or an Excel file. Since our file is a comma-separated file (.csv), we select the first option ("from text file, clipboard or URL...").

This will bring up a box as shown in the second screen of Figure 7.9. In that box, we can specify several options for importing our data file. For instance, we could specify a certain name for our data (but nothing is lost by keeping the default name of "Dataset"), we could check whether or not our dataset contains variable names (the file SoftdrinkSales.csv contains variable names in the first row, so we

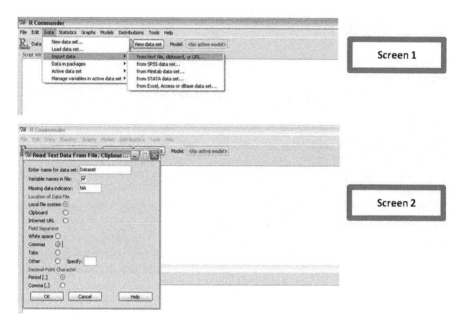

Fig. 7.9 Importing data into the R Commander.

should keep this box checked), we could indicate how missing records are identified in our data (since `SoftdrinkSales.csv` does not have any missing records, this option is irrelevant), and we could specify the location of the file (most of the time this will be "Local file system," as the file will be saved on our hard drive). The most important option is the "Field Separator"; since our file is comma-separated, we should be sure to check the option "Commas." The last option ("Decimal-Point Character") is only relevant if our data originated from, Europe, for example, where commas (rather than periods) signify the start of the decimal places (our file was assembled according to US conventions, so decimal places are indicated by periods – we should be sure to keep "Period" checked). That's it – click on "OK" and you will see a window that will ask you to browse for your data file.

Once you have imported your data, you can start to analyze it. Cautious analysts will first want to look at the data to make sure all information got imported according to their expectations. This can be done by clicking the "View data set" button in the Rcmdr window; the result should be similar to the one in Figure 7.10 (screen 1).

Now you are ready to explore the full power of Rcmdr. Initially, the most useful tabs are the "Data" tab and the "Graphs" tab at the top of the Rcmdr. For instance, if you click on the "Graphs" tab, then you will see several options for graphing you data. Locate the option for "Scatterplot" and see if you can reproduce the scatterplot shown in the second screen of Figure 7.10.

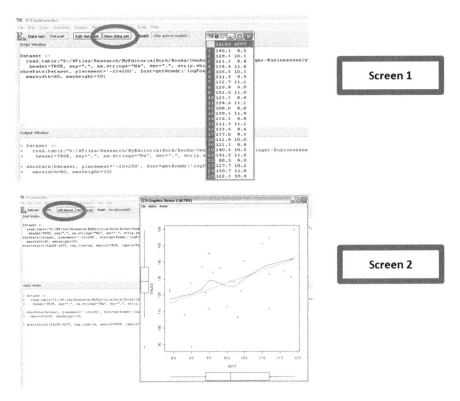

Fig. 7.10 Exploring data in the R Commander.

7.6.2   Rattle

Rattle is another powerful R GUI. In fact, Rattle is specifically geared toward the data mining task and as such it is organized a little bit differently from Rcmdr. We will see this very soon.

The first step is to download Rattle and all the packages that it uses. Rattle uses many different R packages and combines them into one single user interface – this is one reason why it is so powerful. The process of downloading and installing Rattle is similar to that for Rcmdr; however, since Rattle draws on so many different packages, there is more than one step. The first step consists of downloading and installing the package "RGtk2"; this can be done by typing the following line into the R Console window:

```
install.packages(''RGtk2'');
```

(Don't forget to hit "Enter" after typing the command above.) Next we install Rattle and all packages that it depends on; this is done by typing the command

```
install.packages(''rattle'', dependencies=TRUE);
```

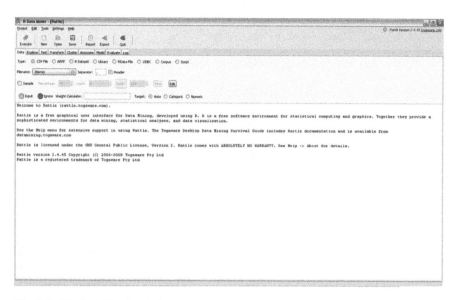

Fig. 7.11 The initial Rattle window.

This process will take quite a while, and you will notice the amount of different packages that Rattle is installing. Make sure that your Internet connection does not get interrupted during this process; otherwise, you may have to start the entire process all over again from the beginning.

After you have downloaded and installed Rattle, you have to activate it for the current session. This is (again) done by typing

```
library(rattle);
```

However, in contrast to Rcmdr, a second step is necessary: you also have to type

```
rattle();
```

and finally the rattle window will appear. This window should resemble the window in Figure 7.11.

Let's import the soft drink sales data from Section 7.4 into Rattle. To that end, locate the Rattle "Data" tab (which is the first Rattle tab). By default, Rattle expects a comma-separated file (notice that the option "CSV File" is prechecked). Now, let's click on the box "Filename"; this will bring up a window that allows you to browse for your file. Locate the file SoftdrinkSales.csv on your hard drive and then click "Open." You are not quite done yet: click on the "Execute" button in the top left corner of the Rattle window – the result should look like the screenshot in Figure 7.12.

A quick comment on Rattle's "Execute" button: All processes and analyses in Rattle are followed by the "Execute" button. In other words, you are never quite finished until you have hit that button; selecting options on the different tabs and/or

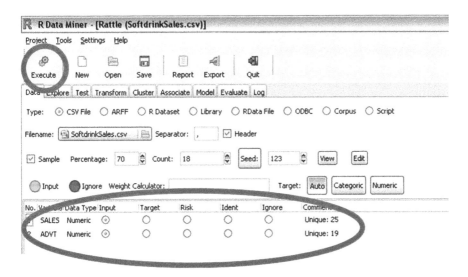

Fig. 7.12 The Rattle window after importing the soft drink sales data.

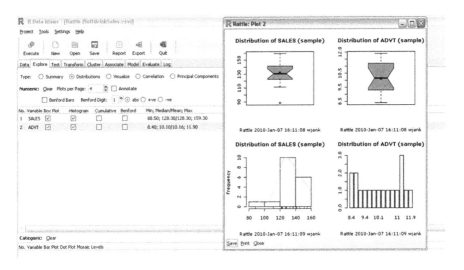

Fig. 7.13 Exploring data in Rattle.

browsing for data files will only become active and relevant *after* you have hit that button. Rattle does not execute any of your commands until that button is activated.

Figure 7.12 shows the result of your data import into Rattle. At the bottom of the window (highlighted by the red oval), Rattle summarizes the data it just imported for you: it displays the data type (which is all numeric in our case), and it allows you to specify which of the variables you consider *input* variables, which ones you consider the *target* variable, which variables denote a case identifier ("Ident"), and which variables you wish to ignore altogether. Input and target variables will become important later on as our modeling efforts strive for predicting the target variable using a combination of different input variables.

You are now in a position to unleash the power of Rattle onto your data. You could start, for example, by exploring your data. This can be done by selecting the "Explore" tab. For instance, you could explore the distributions of the two variables "SALES" and "ADVT" in `SoftdrinkSales.csv`. To that end, select the radio button "Distributions". You will see several options for plotting distributions; see if you can reproduce the histograms and boxplots shown in Figure 7.13.

Index